God B.C.

God's Grace in the Old Testament

— ANTHONY PHILLIPS —

Sacristy
Press

Sacristy Press
PO Box 612, Durham, DH1 9HT

www.sacristy.co.uk

First published in 1977 by Oxford University Press.
Second (revised) edition published 2018 by Sacristy Press, Durham.

Sacristy Limited, registered in England & Wales, number 7565667

British Library Cataloguing-in-Publication Data
A catalogue record for the book is available from the British Library

ISBN 978-1-910519-83-7

For my grandson Luke,
son of my daughter Lucy,
to whom the first edition of God B.C. was dedicated

Foreword

From the first edition, 1977

When St Paul wrote his letters, the gospels had not yet been written and the New Testament did not exist. When, therefore, he commends the study of the scriptures, he is referring to the Old Testament. He tells the young churches, consisting mainly of Gentiles, that the ancient Jewish scriptures are of importance and that God intended them for Christians.

This message is true today. In recent years the Old Testament has been neglected. We need to re-discover what it has to say to us so that it may prove to be profitable in leading God's people along the way to perfection, and the practice of good works.

I warmly commend this book by Dr Phillips, especially to those who during Lent want to deepen their understanding of the Christian faith.

Gerald London:

Gerald Ellison
Bishop of London, 1973–1981

Preface

God B.C. was originally published in 1977. It was an attempt to understand how the Hebrews developed their ideas about the nature of their God as revealed in the Hebrew Scriptures known to Christians as the Old Testament. I argued for a linear process from a God whose love was limited by the response of his people to his demands to one who could not reject them whatever they did, as ultimately and definitively revealed in Jesus Christ. Importantly, though the word "grace" is never used in the Old Testament, I pointed out that, before the Christ event, the Jews already understood their God as one whose very nature prevented him from ever renouncing his love for his "chosen people", who have continued to witness to that love despite centuries of persecution, often at Christian hands.

As would be expected in any discipline, Old Testament studies have gone through many twists and turns in the last forty years. Much has been of a very negative nature, in particular an unwillingness to make concrete assertions about the history and theology of the pre-exilic period. Not unnaturally, some of this criticism has affected the conclusions I drew in *God B.C.* Nonetheless, while wanting to modify the traditional way in which for decades the Pentateuch, the first five books of the Old Testament, has been understood to reach its present form, and above all the linear development of the Hebrews' understanding of their God as set out in *God B.C.*, I still believe we can offer a coherent picture of the history of thought about God and his relationship to humankind as revealed in the Hebrew Scriptures and confirmed in the Christian ones.

It has, of course, long been recognised that the Pentateuch is a composite work, the subject of addition, re-writing and re-editing, though there is no unanimity among scholars as to how it reached its present form. The original proponents of its literary make-up saw it as the product of four sources, J, E, D, and P.

The earliest source J was associated with the early years of the Davidic monarchy and, although many would question such an early ascription, I shall argue that it formed the document of title for the new Davidic state. This source was labelled J as it used the Hebrew proper name for God, Yahweh, which in Germany, where the theory originated, is spelt with a J.

After the division of the Davidic kingdom on Solomon's death (922 BC), it was held that in the northern kingdom another source evolved, labelled E from the use throughout of the generic name for God, *elohim*. I do not myself believe that there is sufficient material to establish such an independent connected source. Rather, it seems to me that, on the fall of the northern kingdom to Assyria (721) and Hezekiah's reform, a radical revision of the J source was undertaken by southern theologians attempting to come to terms with this catastrophe and as a warning to southern Judah that a similar fate could await her.

In the latter years of the Davidic monarchy following Josiah's reform, a completely new work, Deuteronomy (D), was composed. This was used to preface the account of Israel's "history" from entry into the land of Canaan to the Babylonian conquest and its aftermath (Joshua, Judges, 1 and 2 Samuel, 1 and 2 Kings), intended to explain why things happened as they did.

Then, probably during the exile in Babylon, the already revised J account was subjected to a further revision by priestly authors (P) which resulted in the Tetrateuch (Genesis, Exodus, Leviticus, Numbers). Following the return from exile, this work was combined with Deuteronomy and, with some further editing, became the Pentateuch.

In this book, I do not intend to refer to the sources of the Pentateuch by the letters J, E, D, and P. Rather, I shall describe these sources as the document of title associated with the united monarchy of David and Solomon, later redacted following Hezekiah's reform, Deuteronomy and the priestly work.

I know from my own life that one's understanding of God is directly affected by events which happen to us from outside, some wonderful and enhancing, others hideous and soul destroying. So I believe it was for the Hebrews. Reacting to what happened to them historically, the authors of their Scriptures assessed anew their relationship to their God, editing and adding to earlier writings. Rather than a gradual linear development, I believe that two of these events, the loss of the northern kingdom of Israel to the Assyrians in 721 and of the southern kingdom of Judah to the Babylonians in 586, led to mistaken conclusions limiting God's love, which the experience of the exile and return to their land corrected and was for Christians even more generously confirmed in the Christ event. As with our own lives, it is always a temptation to faith in the generosity of God to draw the wrong conclusions in adversity and limit or even renounce his love, particularly in the face of the inexplicable or his apparent absence.

Inevitably in this reassessment of my previous thoughts on Old Testament theology, I shall draw on already published material, not only in *God B.C.* but in other of my books and articles, though the result is a thoroughly new and fuller presentation of the issues first tackled in *God B.C.* Quotations of biblical references are from the *Revised English Bible* (1989; "REB"). The quotations from Ibsen's play *Brand* are from Michael Meyer's translation (1960, New York). All dates are BC, or, as now sometimes written, BCE, that is before the Common Era.

Anthony Phillips
January 2018

Contents

CHAPTER 1

The Origins of Israel

i. The Emergence of Israel

The origins of Israel remain a matter of scholarly dispute. Before the emergence of the Davidic-Solomonic empire, Canaan was made up of a series of independent city states nominally at least subject to Egyptian domination. But from the fourteenth-century Tell el-Amarna letters, it is clear that Egypt was already losing her grip over her eastern empire. Part of this diplomatic correspondence, discovered at Tell el-Amarna in Egypt, consists of a series of appeals from the kings of the small Canaanite city states for Egyptian help in the face of attacks from roving bands of *Habiru,* a word widely believed to be related to "Hebrew". These *Habiru* were not an ethnic group but a social one, and seem to have been refugees or people on the margins of society, disaffected and acting outside the existing political system. They survived by becoming mercenaries, robbers or brigands. So, in one letter, the Governor of Jerusalem, an Egyptian appointee, expresses to his overlords anxiety about the depredations brought about by the *Habiru.*

These *Habiru* are not, though, the only force referred to in Egyptian texts at that time. We also encounter the *Shasu,* found over a wide area but in particular in the region occupied by the Edomites, that area of the *Negeb* around Petra in the south of modern Jordan. They appear to have been organised in tribes which were both sedentary and nomadic.

These texts also refer to "Yahweh in the land of the *Shasu*", which seems to indicate that Yahweh, who was eventually to become the sole God of the Hebrews, was originally associated with that mountainous region occupied by the *Shasu*. Indeed, Yahweh is described as coming "forth from Seir" (Judges 5:4), the other name for that region occupied by the Edomites, and is associated with Teman and Mount Paran, both located in territory south of Judah (Habakkuk 3:3).

Further leaving aside for a moment the historicity of the exodus, Moses too is to be associated with this region, being particularly attached to Midian, again a people rather than a place, located on the fringes of the *Negeb,* that area where the *Shasu* were particularly active. It was there at the burning bush that Moses first encountered the deliverer God, Yahweh (Exodus 3). He is alleged to have married a Midianite (Exodus 2:21). He may well have been a significant local figure, possibly even connected with the local sanctuary. The poem in Habbakuk also refers to "the tent curtains of Midian" (Habakkuk 3:7).

That Yahweh was not an indigenous god of Canaan is confirmed by the fact that nowhere is he found within the Canaanite pantheon. Further tradition holds that the land was not the Israelites' by inheritance, but by the gift of Yahweh (Deuteronomy 4:1).

What is clear is that the main interest of imperial Egypt's foreign policy was the coastal plain of Palestine, the corridor to Mesopotamia. The sparsely populated hill country was of little concern, save in so far as it might fall into hostile hands. It was governed by local rulers who, with various degrees of commitment, gave allegiance to Pharaoh. It was in this hilly region away from the attention of imperial power that, as archaeology has confirmed, considerable movements of population occurred in the late Bronze Age.

While we will never be able to know precisely how Israel emerged as a nation, the evidence outlined above seems to indicate that a number of distinctive elements, including the disaffected indigenous *Habiru* and the nomadic *Shasu*, eventually joined forces in the hill country of Palestine under a new God, Yahweh, introduced into the land by the *Shasu*. At the same time, the invasion of the coastal plain around 1200 by the Philistines, part of the Sea Peoples originating from the Aegean basin, together with the emergence of a new political entity in the hill country, sounded the death knell of the eastern Egyptian empire. It would be with these Philistines, who, unlike the indigenous Hebrews, had a properly equipped army (1 Samuel 13:19–22) which included chariots, that Saul and David would principally be concerned. The fact that no trace of a Philistine language has survived indicates the rapidity of their integration into Canaan. They retained their distinctiveness in the Semitic world by remaining uncircumcised. Ironically, they would give their name to the land in which they settled—Palestine.

Confirmation that by the late thirteenth century Israel was emerging as a political reality is provided by the Egyptian Merneptah Stele, dated around 1220. This records the Egyptians' victory over the Libyans, but has tacked on to it references to victories in Syria and Palestine. Some scholars have doubted the authenticity of these latter assertions, for the Egyptian myth of the invincible Pharaoh often led to grandiose claims of victory over enemies which cannot be reconciled with historical evidence. But whether or not there was a Palestinian campaign, what is important is that the stele refers to Israel as a people, rather than a country, the Egyptians had encountered in Canaan.

Clearly, the stele indicates some kind of unification of the peoples of the hill country, though the fact that they are described as a people rather than a land would confirm that they were not yet a nation. This would be brought about by David.

The Bible itself reflects the process by which various tribes gradually attained political and juridical unification culminating in the Davidic monarchy. This is the significance of the judges described in the biblical book of that name, of whom Samuel appears to have been the last representative. While their authority seems to have been extended over a fairly limited geographical area, the process of centralisation was now irreversible.

Already, three kingdoms had been established in Transjordan— Ammon, Moab and Edom—all of whom were at times to show interest in the land to the west. In this new world of emerging states, if the tribes of the Judaean hills were to keep their independence, then they must follow suit and embrace nationhood.

There can be no doubt that what accelerated this process was the settlement of the Philistines on the coastal plain and their attempt to move up into the hill country. By the time of Samuel these Philistines had already successfully infiltrated inland, establishing garrisons and threatening the embryonic coalition of tribes which would eventually become Israel as they attempted to bring about united rule over the whole area. Only a larger coalition under an acknowledged leader could effectively meet this threat.

During the tenth century, a dramatic move from largely rural settlements to urban centres took place. Archaeology has confirmed that many villages were abandoned. This was a gradual process only reaching its culmination with the full establishment of the Solomonic state with its necessary administrative bureaucracy. For to achieve statehood, the people had first to evolve an ethnic identity eventually realised in a common language, culture and religion. Largely, this was the work of Solomon once David had, through various military campaigns, secured the territory that was to become Israel. It was David's genius after the failure of Saul that ensured the establishment of the line which, after its demise following the Babylonian conquest and exile in 586, would become the basis of Israel's Messianic hope, the realisation of which, for Christians in the Christ event, will conclude this revisited study of my original *God B.C.*

ii. The Exodus

To explain the origins of Israel without reference to the exodus may seem idiosyncratic to some. But startling as it may seem, outside the Hebrew Scriptures there is no independent account of this "event". Egyptian records make no mention of the loss of the Egyptians' first born sons, including Pharaoh's heir, of their Hebrew workforce on whom they were said to be reliant for their building programme, of their wealth allegedly pillaged by the escaping Hebrews, and of their entire army in a dramatic drowning in the Red Sea. Yet no hint of economic or military disaster surfaces in Egypt. And despite the thousands of texts discovered and hundreds of sites excavated, no evidence has been found for Israel's presence in Egypt.

Neither is there any need here to examine in detail the surrealist nature of the account, as a study of the numbers involved confirms. Long ago, Bishop Colenso pointed out that the marching column of the fleeing Hebrews would have been twenty miles long and six yards wide, sacrificial lambs would have had to be killed at a rate of 1,250 lambs a minute, and each priest would have had to sprinkle the blood of 333 lambs a minute for two hours together. To the horror of the prudish Victorians, he even commented on the problems of relieving the calls of nature for such a number.

What needs to be appreciated, and this is true of both Testaments, is that the Hebrews did their theology by story in which basic truths about God are presented clothed as historical events.

At the heart of the exodus narrative lies a miracle on a gigantic scale which is designed to confirm that Israel owes her existence to the saving act of her God alone. In effect, it acts as a confession of faith, not just in God's past actions, but for both present and future generations of his "chosen people".

As we shall see later, the narrative is a composite work, the product of various authors/editors at different points in Israel's history, when Israel's faith needed to be reassessed in the changed circumstances in which she found herself. Any attempt to explain the narrative through natural causes in order to make it historically credible only succeeds in making it less remarkable from a theological standpoint.

The whole purpose of the narrative is to act as a prototype of salvation. It recognises the Hebrew God as the sole agent of deliverance. Only in his service can his people find the freedom which "in setting out from Egypt" is theirs to embrace. As an early Rabbinic saying puts it: "Every Jew is to think of himself as actually taking part in the exodus itself." Asking whether the story of the exodus is fact or fiction misses the point. It is neither. It is, though, reality for all who are prepared to risk themselves in it and, like the Hebrews of the narrative, find a future of which hitherto they had hardly dared to dream. Faith evolves in history, but is not verifiable by history.

The establishment of the state was the first "event" which forced the newly-born Israel to consider how she stood with her God. This was the purpose of the first literary strand which lies behind the complex literary work known as the Pentateuch, and to Jews as the Torah. By giving the new state its document of title, it confirmed Israel's election as God's "chosen people".

In order to unite all the disparate elements brought under the new monarch's protection, every available tradition was used. One batch of tales told of an ancestor called Abraham whose memory lived on in Beersheba and the *Negeb* in the south. Another centred around a leader known as Jacob associated with the northern highlands, Bethel and Shechem. But a third concerned those who were not natives of the land, but who entered it from outside, bringing with them allegiance to their God Yahweh who, for all the disparate groups uniting to form Israel, was seen as the liberator and by whose grace alone they possessed the land. And what better way of uniting these various traditions than by telling a tale involving a family whose origins lay outside Israel but whose ancestor was promised the land (Genesis 13:28) whose boundaries now formed the Davidic kingdom and whose possession was ultimately due to the humiliation of the imperial power which had for so long dominated the Palestinian landscape.

So the narrative of the patriarchs Abraham, Isaac and Jacob was formed, culminating in Joseph's sale and journey to Egypt, from where years later Moses would bring the Israelites through the desert to allow Joshua to "conquer" the land of Canaan which God willed to them. Thereby the Davidic state acquired its document of title. The land belonged to them, even if in fact it had been acquired very differently. And every citizen knew that his ancestor had a part in its creation. It was a united kingdom.

iii. The Prologue

The author of this first literary work prefaced his account with a prologue which was intended to achieve two things. He delineated first what it was to be human and second that God could never renounce that humankind for which he was responsible, no matter what infamy they committed.

The opening chapters of Genesis are a composite work made up of the writing of the author who gave the Davidic state its document of title and, as we shall see much later in this study, a later addition to the earlier work in the light of Israel's exile in Babylon in 586. That Genesis 1–11 is the product of different authors is not difficult to see, even in an English translation of the Hebrew text. For example, while the later seven-day creation account (Genesis 1–2:4a) adopts a formal, almost liturgical, style, the language being dignified and God remaining distant and transcendent, the much earlier Eden narrative (Genesis 2:4b–3:24) depicts God in intimate human terms.

This is not as shocking as might at first appear. For we shall see that the much later writing was in fact designed to reaffirm the earlier one, whose theology had been wrongly rejected and needed to be reasserted at the lowest point in Israel's history.

At the beginning of his narrative, the author of Israel's document of title describes the creation of the first man and woman, who are set in a paradisal garden in which there are two trees whose fruit they are forbidden to eat. One is the tree of life, the other is the tree of the knowledge of good and evil. These trees designate the difference between God and humankind.

In the first place, humans are mortal. While in some other ancient creation stories the man is pictured as losing his immortality, in the Genesis account there is no suggestion that humankind was ever intended by God to be immortal. Man (adam) was taken from earth (adamah) and to earth he will return.

Second, men and women cannot know as God knows. The meaning of "the knowledge of good and evil", the title of the other tree, is the knowledge of all things, the kind of knowledge that only God can have as he is outside the system that he has made. Men and women placed within the system, while free to explore every aspect of creation, cannot get beyond it. Their knowledge is of necessity limited. So for instance, as we shall see from the Book of Job, some issues, such as an explanation for unjust suffering, are outside their realm of knowledge. But there is no conflict with science. The first man is specifically commissioned to order God's creation, over which he is given dominion as tenant of the garden.

The author of the document of title then goes on to describe a succession of events of ever-increasing audacity whereby humans challenge the limit God has imposed on them. Why should they not be the equal of their creator? Yet while every act of rebellion results in terrible disorder, God cannot renounce them.

In an attempt to gain the same understanding as God, the first man eats the forbidden fruit and chaos results. And although God clothes the couple's nakedness, the result is expulsion of the man and woman from the garden (Genesis 3). There then follows the total breakdown in human relationships as Cain murders his brother Abel, taking possession of his blood which, like all blood, the Hebrews saw as belonging to God. But lest God's work in creation be brought to nothing, the murderer is given divine protection (Genesis 4). Yet disorder so increases that it even goes beyond the confines of the earth to involve the divine world (Genesis 6:1–4). Therefore, God determines to start afresh: the family of Noah is chosen to survive the flood (parts of Genesis 6–9). Even this divine purge cannot bring humankind to heel. Their arrogant ambition to be like God knows no bounds as they build their tower seeking to penetrate the divine realm itself (Genesis 11:1–9). Again, human arrogance is followed by chaos as God confuses their language. But God is not to be defeated: he turns from punishment to salvation and calls Abraham, in whom all the nations of the earth will bless themselves (Genesis 12:1–3).

The importance of this first author's prologue to his work is that it shows that God is utterly committed to his project, no matter what humankind can throw at him. While disobedience to God inevitably leads to chaos, God will not abandon humankind but provides a way forward, hope for the future, a future of which in God's mind there is no doubt.

iv. The Call of Abraham

After his introductory prologue, the author begins his main work with the call of Abraham (Genesis 12:1–3), whom the reader is to identify with David, as only at the time of the united monarchy were all the significant sites which figure in the patriarchal narratives simultaneously occupied by the Hebrews. Indeed, both Genesis 13 and 28 mirror the empire of the new Davidic state. And while in Genesis 12 God promises Abraham that he will make his name great, in 2 Samuel 7 the same promise is made to David.

The author's election theology is most clearly spelt out in Genesis 15. First God promises the childless Abraham that he will have descendants as numerous as the stars:

> Abram replied, "Lord God, what can you give me, seeing that I am childless? The heir to my household is Eliezer of Damascus. You have given me no children, and so my heir must be a slave born in my house". The word of the Lord came to him: "This man will not be your heir; your heir will be a child of your own body". He brought Abram outside and said: "Look up at the sky, and count the stars, if you can. So many will your descendants be".
>
> *Genesis 15:2–5*

God then ratifies his promise by ordering Abraham to bring him various animals and birds. The animals are cut in two and the parts placed opposite each other. At dusk, a deep sleep falls on Abraham (the same sleep that fell on the man when woman was created) and God in the form of a smoking pot and a flaming torch walks between the divided carcasses. What is happening is that God is sealing his promise of election in the traditional way. When two parties made an agreement, they divided animals and together walked between them, so signifying that if either broke the contract then he would be slaughtered like the divided animals. But God's agreement with Abraham is one-sided. Only one party does the walking: only God commits himself. The election of Abraham and his descendants, the election of Israel, is unconditional. It is therefore no surprise that, at the high point of the narrative, the promise to Abraham is fulfilled in like manner with God's commitment that David and his heirs will reign for ever:

> Your family and your kingdom will be established for ever in my sight; your throne will endure for all time.
>
> **2 Samuel 7:16**
> *(cf. 2 Samuel 23:5; Psalm 89:3, 28, 34; Psalm 132:12)*

Neither with Abraham nor David does God make any demands, but commits himself without reserve to them and their successors.

This then is the author's theological understanding of the nature of the Hebrew God, a God who without reservation has committed himself for all time to humankind, but through whom his chosen people would bring blessing to all nations (Genesis 12:1–3). Nothing on Israel's part threatens that relationship though, as her history will show, failure of commitment to her God can have dire consequences but not ultimate rejection.

While the patriarchal stories will again acquire a new importance in the exilic period, when additions will be made to the original narrative as they were to the prologue to Genesis, a number of factors confirm that they can be regarded as an integral part of the first literary work, Israel's document of title.

First, in contrast to the nomadism of the open country, Genesis indicates that the patriarchs occupied a clearly defined territory in immediate proximity to a settled urban population, so forming an economic unit whose prosperity depended on the continued presence of both parties. While conditions in Palestine up to the end of the second millennium would have encouraged such economic interdependence, they would certainly not have existed as late as the exilic period. Yet it is recognition that such a dimorphic society underlies the patriarchal narratives that explains a number of factors to which scholars have often drawn attention as at variance with nomadism in the open country. These include the description of Abraham as a resident alien, the importance of land inheritance, the method of agriculture employed by the patriarchs, the many references to camping in the vicinity of towns, and the easy social and economic relations with their inhabitants.

Second, it has been argued that the emphasis on the promise of land indicates that Israel's possession of that land was under threat, so pointing to the immediate pre-exilic or exilic period. But examination of the promise indicates that it is always framed as a formal legal transfer of realty (Genesis 12:7, 13:15, 15:18, 24:7, 28:13). This must mean that the promise is being used to justify Israel's actual possession of what was known by the author to have been another's land. He is anxious to give Israel a valid document of title. Her possession was "legal". The land has been properly conveyed to her. Clearly such an assertion would have been all important to the new Davidic monarchy conscious of the land's Canaanite past.

Third, unlike the prophets or the Book of Deuteronomy, the patriarchal narratives contain no criticism or polemic against Canaanite religion associated with Baal. This would reflect the pro-Canaanizing process of the early monarchic period as Canaanite sanctuaries, their cult and personnel were taken over together with the indigenous agricultural festivals, Yahweh being substituted for Baal as Israel's deity (cf. Psalm 29). So David took over the Jebusite city of Jerusalem and Solomon built his temple there with Tyrian help, placing it under the authority of the former Canaanite priest Zadok. Further, it has now been generally recognised that the distinctions between Canaanite and "authorised" Israelite religion were far less rigid than the Bible would have us believe.

Fourth, while later belief that the law on sacrifice contained in the Book of Leviticus was given to Moses at Sinai, thereby preventing any reference to the patriarchs offering sacrifices in later additions to the original narrative, the earlier author had no such inhibitions. Nor are they restricted to Jerusalem as the later reform of King Josiah required, the patriarchs being recorded as sacrificing at numerous different sites. Indeed, the earlier author is able to justify Israel's possession of both Palestine and her cultic sites of non-Hebrew origin by linking them to the patriarchs.

We can then conclude this part of our assessment of Israel's understanding of her God by reaffirming that the physical and theological map with which this first author who gave Israel her document of title was working was the map of his own time, into which he set the traditions of the past in order to proclaim his unshakeable faith in the future. The author celebrates the unqualified election of Israel as the fulfilment of the history process from creation itself through the patriarchal and exodus narratives resulting in the Davidic state, and saw that process continuing on to a glorious future. It was left to outside events to disrupt such optimism and lead to a new and unfortunate assessment of the nature of Israel's relations with her God.

v. The Law

This account is very different from that presented in my original *God B.C.* There I argued that at the heart of Israel's relationship with her God was the covenant inaugurated at Sinai. From her inception, Israel's continued existence was conditional, being dependent on her obedience to God's law. God of his grace had elected her to be his chosen people: but in return he had placed the strict obligations of the covenant upon her. Failure to comply would lead to punishment, even abandonment.

But research has now conclusively shown that the two-way covenant concept between God and Israel, with the threat of Israel's total rejection by God, has no place in the earliest narrative of Exodus, but was introduced as a result of subsequent historical events that caused Israel mistakenly to re-evaluate her theology, leading to a misunderstanding of the nature of her God.

What then can we now say about the law? Certainly, the embryonic Davidic state would need provisions to be applied universally throughout the kingdom. Probably they are reflected in the legal precedents known as The Book of the Covenant and contained in Exodus 21–22:16. A number of these are concerned with distinguishing the crime of murder from the civil offence of assault. In my view, from its inception ancient Israel recognised the difference between civil wrongs against particular individuals, for which damages were paid to the injured party, and crimes, that is offences against the community, which the community punished in its own name. In pre-exilic Israel this took the form of stoning to death.

As an example, Exodus 21:18–19 deals with the question of a time limitation against a possible charge of murder:

> When men quarrel and one hits another with a stone or with his fist, and the man is not killed but takes to his bed, and if he recovers so as to walk about outside with his staff, then the one who struck him has no liability, except that he must pay compensation for the other's loss of time and see that his recovery is complete.

Once the injured man has gone for a walk without human aid, his assailant can no longer be charged with murder, even if his victim should die on the next day. Instead, damages for assault must now be assessed, which amount to compensation for the victim's enforced idleness and his medical expenses. Since his family would receive no damages if the assault became murder, and the assailant would himself be executed (Exodus 21:12), it was in the interests of all parties that the victim should recover.

This distinction between civil and criminal offences underlies Nathan's famous parable told after David's adultery with Bathsheba and Uriah's subsequent murder (2 Samuel 12). This turns on the fact that theft of property was not regarded as a crime but a civil offence for which damages could compensate the victim, though in the case of animals, as a deterrent, such damages were punitive:

> When a man steals an ox or a sheep and slaughters or sells it, he must repay five beasts for the ox and four sheep for the sheep. He must pay in full; if he has no means, he is to be sold to pay for the theft.
>
> *Exodus 22:1–2b*

In highly emotive language, Nathan describes how a rich man with vast flocks seizes a poor man's one ewe lamb to serve up to an unexpected guest. At this David reacts as Nathan expects:

> As the Lord lives, the man who did this deserves to die! He shall
> pay for the lamb four times over, because he has done this and
> shown no pity.
>
> *2 Samuel 12:5b–6*

Since only the civil law had been broken, the only action which could be
taken against the rich man was a suit for damages which, because of his
wealth, left him virtually unpunished. But in David's eyes he deserves to
be treated as a criminal and put to death.

But then comes the climax, when Nathan discloses that David himself
is the rich man of the parable, and that he has not merely committed a
civil offence, but been guilty of the double crime of adultery (Leviticus
20:10; Deuteronomy 22:22) and murder, for which the law demanded
the death penalty. David in fact only escapes such punishment at the
direct pardon of God.

I would then maintain that from her inception as a nation state,
ancient Israel's law had an entirely different attitude to property in
contrast to people, as Nathan's parable confirms. Indeed, I believe that
the commandment on theft (Exodus 20:15; Deuteronomy 5:19) is not
to be interpreted as referring to theft of property, but to man theft, as
spelt out in Deuteronomy 24:7, where the Hebrew describes the thief
as "the stealer of life". This was the fate of Joseph. While property could
be replaced, people could not, and as members of the elect community
they had to be protected by the ultimate sanction of the death penalty.

What though is remarkable is the amount of "legislation" which could
never have been enforced through the courts but depended solely on
compassion, whether towards the poor or those with no legal status—the
widow, orphan or resident alien, even animals—for such compassion
reflected the very nature of the God who of his grace had elected Israel
as his chosen people. For example:

> If you take your neighbour's cloak in pawn, return it to him by
> sunset, because it is his only covering. It is the cloak in which he
> wraps his body; in what else can he sleep? If he appeals to me, I
> shall listen, for I am full of compassion.
>
> *Exodus 22:26*

Because such laws could not be enforced, the only sanction offered is the direct action of God against a disobedient community. Poverty, like widowhood and orphandom, was inevitable, but these were disorderly situations and everything was to be done to alleviate them. To exploit others' misfortunes, even to ignore them, was totally alien to the character of Israel's gracious God, who always valued people above property.

Yet the most effective agent of oppression was the maladministration of law. Consequently, the Book of the Covenant warns against such practice:

> You must not deprive the poor man of justice in his lawsuit. Avoid all lies, and do not cause the death of the innocent and guiltless, for I the Lord will never acquit the guilty. Do not accept a bribe, for bribery makes the discerning person blind and the just person give a crooked answer.
>
> *Exodus 23:6–8*

It is then vital that those who have power should be incorruptible and exercise it impartially, so mirroring the very nature of God himself, the just judge of all humankind.

vi. Conclusion

We can then conclude this discussion of Israel's initial understanding of the nature of her God as a God of grace. Of his free will he had selected her from all the nations of the world. Her unconditional election was assured. The promise to Abraham had been fulfilled in David.

Solomon's glorious reign, in which even Pharaoh thought it diplomatic to marry off one of his daughters to the king of this emerging state, confirmed God's blessing of his people, who could confidently look to the future under the protection of their God, Yahweh, whose temple now graced Jerusalem. True, the law indicated that this God expected his people to adopt certain standards with regard to the poor and underprivileged, but this only served to confirm the generosity of his nature. Even the division of the kingdom on Solomon's death did not dampen such optimism.

It would be outside events prompted by the prophetic movement which would force Israel to rethink her theology and, as a result, picture her God in a very different light.

CHAPTER 2

The Eighth-Century Prophetic Protest

On the death of Solomon, the empire split into the richer northern kingdom of Israel, ruled from Samaria by a succession of different dynasties, and southern Judah, centred on Jerusalem and her temple, which continued to be governed by the Davidic line. Both kingdoms, with varying degrees of enthusiasm, continued to worship Yahweh, whom they believed to have chosen them. He was probably worshipped as a bull God in the northern kingdom and may well have had a consort, Asherah. While monotheism—the belief in only one God—would only be affirmed in the exilic period, Yahweh was nonetheless seen as responsible for the election of his people, no matter in what form he was worshipped and whether other gods were acknowledged.

One difficulty scholars have is that all the material in the Hebrew Scriptures ultimately comes to us through Jerusalem eyes. Though originally it was thought that the northern kingdom produced a parallel document of title to be found within the Pentateuch, sufficient material for a connected narrative can no longer be discerned. Rather, what we shall discover is that the Davidic-Solomonic document of title was radically edited following the fall of the northern kingdom and Judah's reassessment of the nature of her relationship with her God. It is at this point that the threat of Israel's ultimate extinction at God's hands enters Hebrew theology, helped on by the prophets' condemnation of both kingdoms.

It would seem that, from the Hebrews' earliest days in Canaan, prophets, not all of whom were loyal to Yahweh, were active in the religious life of Israel. This was the primary concern of the Elijah/Elisha traditions. Certainly, Yahweh's worship was far from exclusive and syncretism was a regular feature of religious life.

It was in the eighth century that the prophetic movement reached its full fruition in the work of Amos, Micah and Isaiah and, quite distinctively, Hosea. Their concern is the failure of the people to reflect the will of Yahweh, both within the cult and society at large. Neither was independent of the other in Yahweh's eyes. Failure could only result in divine action against the elect people:

> You alone I have cared for among all the nations of the world;
> that is why I shall punish you for all your wrongdoing.
>
> *Amos 3:2*

Although from southern Judah, Amos went north to prophesy in Israel, probably attracted by its greater prosperity, underneath which there was considerable oppression of those who had no means of defending themselves. After a series of oracles denouncing foreign nations for various war crimes (Amos 1:3–2:3), in exactly the same format Amos condemns Israel for the exploitation of those who were not in a position to protect themselves:

> These are the words of the Lord:
> For crime after crime of Israel
> I shall grant them no reprieve,
> because they sell honest folk for silver
> and the poor for a pair of sandals.
> They grind the heads of the helpless into the dust
> and push the humble out of their way.
> Father and son resort to the temple girls,
> so profaning my holy name.
> Men lie down beside every altar
> on garments held in pledge,
> and in the house of their God they drink wine
> on the proceeds of fines.
>
> *Amos 2:6–8*

While scholars have disputed what precise actions were envisaged in these examples of exploitation listed by Amos, it is clear that the prophet was not introducing new ideas, but formally indicting Israel for that kind of conduct which fell within the provisions of humanness and righteousness in the Book of the Covenant (Exodus 22:21–27, 23:1–3, 6–9). As far as God was concerned these were the equivalent of war crimes on his people. His further citations of oppression by the rich and perversion of justice are only similar examples of his original indictment:

> You that turn justice to poison
> and thrust righteousness to the ground,
> you that hate a man who brings the wrongdoer to court
> and abominate him who speaks nothing less than truth.
>
> *Amos 5:7, 10*

So Amos indicates that the only hope for the future lies in the proper administration of justice:

> Hate evil, and love good;
> establish justice in the courts;
> it may be that the Lord, the God of Hosts,
> will show favour to the survivors of Joseph.
>
> *Amos 5:15*

Israel's election made her a unique people. As God had been gracious to her, so she was to mirror that same graciousness within her society, yet she had in fact done the opposite:

> Can horses gallop over rocks?
> Can the sea be ploughed with oxen?
> Yet you have turned into venom the process of law,
> justice itself you have turned into poison.
>
> *Amos 6:12*

Amos is not though springing any surprises. It should have been perfectly obvious that Israelite society was falling short of what Yahweh required

from his people. To confirm this, Amos summons foreign nations who
know nothing of Israel's law to observe what is going on in Samaria.
Even as foreigners they are expected to condemn the oppression and
exploitation which confronts them:

> Upon the palaces of Ashdod
> and upon the palaces of Egypt,
> make this proclamation:
> Assemble on the hills of Samaria,
> look at the tumult seething among her people,
> at the oppression in her midst;
> what do they care for straight dealing
> who hoard in their palaces
> the gains of violence and plundering?
>
> *Amos 3:9-10*

Yet it is clear from reading Amos that outwardly Israel saw herself as
a law-abiding society. Apart from the perversion of justice, there is no
reference to those crimes and civil wrongs for which the law prescribed
the appropriate penalty. Even the business community, to its irritation,
finds itself constrained by the requirement to keep the Sabbath:

> Listen to this, you that grind the poor and suppress the humble
> in the land while you say, "When will the new moon be over so
> that we may sell grain? When will the sabbath be past so that we
> may expose our wheat for sale, giving short measure in the bushel
> and taking overweight in the silver, tilting the scales fraudulently,
> and selling the refuse of the wheat; that we may buy the weak for
> silver and the poor for a pair of sandals?"
>
> *Amos 8:4-6*

The picture Amos presents is of a prosperous people confident that their
prosperity arose from their excessive religious zeal for Yahweh (Amos
4:1; 6:1, 3-6).

Yet for Amos, Israel's religious practice must be rejected for her treatment of the poor and underprivileged indicated that it lacked content. So, with heavy irony, Amos parodies a call to worship:

> Come to Bethel—and infringe my law!
> Come to Gilgal—and infringe it yet more!
> Bring your sacrifices for the morning,
> Your tithes within three days
> Burn your thank-offering without leaven;
> Announce publicly your free-will offerings;
> For that is what you Israelites love to do!
>
> *Amos 4:4–5*

In doing the very things that were ordained as religious duties, the Israelites were in fact sinning, for their actions outside their worship showed that they had no real understanding of the nature of the God whom they sought to please. How could he accept the gifts of those who at the same time exhibited wanton callousness to the deprived of their community? And the fact that those gifts were far more generous than the law prescribed made no difference. Their sacrifices, properly designed to bring about communion between God and men, had precisely the opposite effect:

> I spurn with loathing your pilgrim-feasts;
> I take no pleasure in your sacred ceremonies.
> When you bring me your whole-offerings and your grain-offerings
> I shall not accept them,
> nor pay heed to your shared-offerings of stall-fed beasts.
> Spare me the sound of your songs;
> I shall not listen to the strumming of your lutes.
> Instead let justice flow on like a river
> and righteousness like a never-failing torrent.
>
> *Amos 5:21–24*

The southern prophet Micah exhibits the same concerns as Amos. So he condemns the deprivation of the small country farmers of their real estate by the wealthy and powerful Jerusalem citizens:

> Woe betide those who lie in bed planning
>   evil and wicked deeds,
> and rise at daybreak to do them,
> knowing that they have the power to do evil!
> They covet fields and take them by force;
> if they want a house they seize it;
> they lay hands on both householder and house,
> on a man and all he possesses.
>
> *Micah 2:1–2*

As a result, their victims become part of the landless poor, dependent on others for their maintenance. The prophet also exhibits the same concern for the oppressed:

> But you are not my people;
> you rise up as my enemy to my face,
> to strip the cloaks from travellers who felt safe
> or from men returning from the battle,
> to drive the women of my people from their pleasant homes,
> and rob their children from my glory for ever.
>
> *Micah 2:8–9*

And like Amos, Micah similarly rejects Israel's worship, however extravagant, unless accompanied by right action within the community:

> What shall I bring when I come before the Lord,
> when I bow before God on high?
> Am I to come before him with whole-offerings
> with yearling calves?
> Will the Lord be pleased with thousands of rams
> or ten thousand rivers of oil?

Shall I offer my eldest son for my wrongdoing,
my child for the sin I have committed?
The Lord has told you mortals what is good,
and what it is the Lord requires of you:
only to act justly, to love loyalty,
to walk humbly with your God.

Micah 6:6–8

Religious practice can never act as a cloak to hide society's ills. It is lack of justice within the elect community which concerns the prophets. This does not just mean that the legal system was corrupt, though this was certainly part of their complaint. But justice is a wider concept than the administration of law through the courts. It governs right relationships within society. That the poor are exploited and dependent members of society go without is equally lack of justice. To keep the law in ancient Israel was not a matter of not breaking certain injunctions: it also contained a positive duty to make sure that there should be no one in need. Where disorder had entered into the community—whether or not through the sufferer's own fault—society as a whole had a duty as far as possible to eradicate it, and if that were impossible, to mitigate any suffering that did occur. Failure to do so could only bring God's judgment:

"Listen, you leaders of Jacob, rulers of Israel,
surely it is for you to know what is right,
and yet you hate good and love evil;
you flay the skin of my people
and tear the flesh from their bones."
They devour the flesh of my people,
strip off their skin,
lay bare their bones;
they cut them up like flesh for the pot,
like meat for the cauldron.
Then they will call to the Lord, but he will not answer.
When that time comes he will hide his face from them,
so wicked are their deeds.

Micah 3:1–4

Yet even with both secular and sacred leaders utterly corrupt, the people clearly thought that they were safe under Yahweh's protection:

> Her leaders sell verdicts for a bribe,
> her priests give rulings for payment,
> her prophets practise divination for money,
> yet claim the Lord's authority.
> "Is not the Lord in our midst?" they say.
> "No disaster can befall us."
>
> *Micah 3:11*

There then follows a prophecy foretelling the utter destruction of Jerusalem and her temple:

> Therefore, because of you
> Zion will become a ploughed field,
> Jerusalem a heap of ruins,
> and the temple mount rough moorland.
>
> *Micah 3:12*

But is this genuine Micah? It seems to depict Jerusalem after the Babylonian conquest. One of the problems for scholars is that we know the prophetic works were edited later by those associated with the Book of Deuteronomy. For what has become clear, as we shall see, is that the eighth-century prophets were not calling Israel and Judah back to a long-established covenant, but rather that their prophetic warnings, followed by the utter annihilation of the northern kingdom, led to the development of covenant theology.

The same concerns for humaneness and righteousness are found in Isaiah. So the prophet affirms that Israel's relationship with Yahweh rests not on appropriate performance of cultic rites, but on the proper administration of justice and the protection of the defenceless in society:

> When you hold out your hands in prayer,
> I shall turn away my eyes.

Though you offer countless prayers,
I shall not listen;
there is blood on your hands.
Wash and be clean;
put away your evil deeds far from my sight;
cease to do evil, learn to do good.
Pursue justice, guide the oppressed;
uphold the rights of the fatherless,
and plead the widow's cause.

Isaiah 1:15–17

The prophet graphically spells out the exploitation of the poor and defenceless by the powerful and those in authority:

The Lord opens the indictment against the
elders and officers of his people:
It is you who have ravaged the vineyard;
in your houses are the spoils taken from the poor.
Is it nothing to you that you crush my people
and grind the faces of the poor?

Isaiah 3:14–15

It is clear that the hub of these three prophets' charges is the exploitation of those who have no means of defending themselves and the maladministration of law. Their appeal is to a sense of moral responsibility from those who control society. Scholars have identified this appeal with the concept of natural law, those actions which should be obvious to all, whoever they are, simply on the grounds of their common humanity. That is why Amos can summon foreign powers to judge Israel (Amos 3:9–10). Probably as early as the Davidic state, these principles had been spelt out—but of necessity very generally—in the unenforceable rulings on humaneness and righteousness (Exodus 22:21–27; 23:1–9) attached to the specific and enforceable laws of the Book of the Covenant (Exodus 21:12–22:17). As far as these prophets were concerned, the future wellbeing of the nation under Yahweh depended on adherence to these natural law principles, regardless of cultic practice.

Strikingly different from the other eighth-century prophets, Hosea makes no reference to the poor and needy and the regulations of humaneness and righteousness. Instead, the emphasis of his prophecy falls on Israel's apostasy, summed up in the word "harlotry". The prophetic book begins with God's command to the prophet to take "an unchaste woman as your wife" (Hosea 1:2), and goes on to record the birth of his children, all given symbolic names, leading to Hosea's threat to divorce his wife for her adultery (Hosea 1–3). This serves as a model for Israel's adulterous relationship with other gods. The prophet, meditating on his marriage and Israel's apostasy, alternately moves between passages of condemnation leading to an ending of the relationship, contrasted with oracles of hope and restoration, though once again it is difficult to know how much of the material has been edited by the Deuteronomists. Certainly, there are striking similarities between the books of Hosea and Deuteronomy.

What is clear is that Israel's worship of Yahweh was patchy. The old Canaanite religion associated with the fertility of the land remained very much alive, epitomised by idolatry, illicit sacrifices and cult prostitution:

> They ask advice from a piece of wood
> and accept the guidance of the diviner's wand;
> for a spirit of promiscuity has led them astray
> and they are unfaithful to their God.
> They sacrifice on mountaintops
> and burn offerings on the hills,
> under oak and poplar
> and the terebinth's pleasant shade.
> That is why your daughters turn to prostitution
> and your son's brides commit adultery.
>
> ***Hosea 4:12–13***

Indeed, popular religion may have continued to address Yahweh as Baal. It was therefore important for Hosea to assert that it was Yahweh, not Baal, who brought fertility to the land:

> She does not know that it was I who gave her
> the grain, the new wine, and fresh oil,
> I who lavished on her silver and gold
> which they used for the Baal.

Hosea 2:8

Further, in the northern kingdom, Yahweh appears to have been worshipped as a bull-god:

> Samaria, your calf-god is loathsome!
> My anger burns against them!
> How long must they remain guilty?
> The calf was made in Israel;
> a craftsman fashioned it and it is no god;
> it will be reduced to splinters.

Hosea 8:5-6

It is failure of knowledge of Yahweh that leads to Israel's condemnation, for which there will be no escape in political alliances (Hosea 5:13-14; 7:11-13; 8:9-10). The charge against her is damning:

> There is no good faith or loyalty,
> no acknowledgment of God in the land.

Hosea 4:1b

Israel entirely lacks that kind of intense loyalty expected of every intimate relationship. As a result, punishment is inevitable:

> Therefore the land will be desolate
> and all who live in it will languish,
> with the wild beasts and the birds of the air;
> even the fish shall vanish from the sea.

Hosea 4:3

The intervening verse is clearly designed to define what conduct actually constituted lack of "good faith or loyalty" and "acknowledgment", and is probably an interpolation for neither the rest of Hosea's prophecy, nor that of his fellow prophet to the north, Amos, points to that state of general chaos described in this verse:

> People swear oaths and break them;
> they kill and rob and commit adultery;
> there is violence, one deed of blood after another.
>
> *Hosea 4:2*

It would seem that specific criminal law provisions are being used theologically as a blanket expression to indicate total rejection of Yahweh ("rob" should again be interpreted as man theft), which for the interpolator justifies the fall of Samaria to Assyria. These criminal law offences reflect the criminal law provisions in the Decalogue and were probably later introduced into the prophecy of Hosea to confirm the justness of Yahweh's action against Samaria.

Yet for Hosea himself, knowing the fullness of God's love makes the annihilation of Israel seem an impossibility:

> How can I hand you over, Ephraim,
> how can I surrender you, Israel?
> How can I make you like Admah
> or treat you as Zeboyim?
> A change of heart moves me,
> tenderness kindles within me.
> I am not going to let loose my fury,
> I shall not turn and destroy Ephraim,
> for I am God, not a mortal;
> I am the Holy One in your midst.
> I shall not come with threats.
>
> *Hosea 11:8-9*

Two unique features occur in Hosea's prophecy. First, in parallel with "my *torah* (law)", Hosea refers to "my *berit* (covenant)":

They have violated my covenant
and rebelled against my instruction.

Hosea 8:1b

Here *torah,* translated as "instruction" in the REB, is being used in
the sense of the complete expression of Yahweh's will. This is how it is
understood in Deuteronomy. It has therefore been argued that this usage,
as well as the reference to "covenant", indicates that this is a Deuteronomic
insertion indicating the breach of the covenant inaugurated at Sinai. But
I shall argue that it was in reaction to the fall of the northern kingdom
(721) that the concept of covenant entered Hebrew theology and that it
was at the time of Hezekiah's reform that this concept was inserted into
the Exodus Sinai narrative. It is therefore entirely possible that Hosea
was the first to use the term *berit* to spell out the relationship between
Yahweh and Israel, particularly in view of his rejection of appeals to
foreign powers for help, which, as we shall see, the covenant concept
ruled out.

Hosea 8:1 is not the only occurrence of *berit* in Hosea's prophecy:

At Admah they violated my covenant,
there they played me false.

Hosea 6:7

This further strengthens the case that Hosea could have been the
originator of the use of "covenant" to designate Israel's relationship with
her God.

The other unique feature in Hosea's prophecy is the negative use
of I AM to describe Yahweh, though this is never made clear in any
mainstream translation of the Bible that I know:

Call him Lo-ammi;
for you are not my people,
and I shall not be your God.

Hosea 1:9

Literally, the last line should be rendered "and I am no I AM to you".

The derivation of Yahweh's name from the verb "to be" is spelt out in Exodus 3:14 and it is usually assumed that Hosea was drawing on the Exodus narrative. But the Exodus account has widely been recognised as overloaded. To Moses' question asking God how he should answer the people when they ask for his name, God apparently supplies more than one answer:

> God answered, "I AM that I am. Tell them that I AM has sent you to them". He continued, "You are to tell the Israelites that it is the Lord, the God of their forefathers, the God of Abraham, Isaac, and Jacob, who has sent you to them. This is my name for ever; this is my title in every generation".
>
> **Exodus 3:14–15**

Clearly, the original author's concern was to identify the God of the fathers with the God who had appeared to Moses at the burning bush (Exodus 3:1–12). He is bringing together in his document of title traditions associated with the indigenous people of the land, with those entering it bringing their God Yahweh with them.

If this is the case, then verse 15 is the original answer to Moses' question. The use of the first person singular of the verb "to be" in verse 14 is then a later interpolation which explains the meaning of the divine name Yahweh. Why was it felt necessary to insert it?

In all probability the source for this interpolation lies in the account of the naming of Hosea's third child and the negative use of I AM (Hosea 1:9). But the interpolator, in deriving God's name from the verb "to be", is not primarily concerned with etymology but theology. He is reaffirming that Yahweh is still Israel's God.

As we shall see, the interpolation of verse 14 is all part of the radical reappraisal of the Exodus narrative in view of the fall of the northern kingdom to Assyria and the introduction of covenant theology modelled on the form of the ancient suzerainty treaty common to Israel's neighbours, to which southern Judah would become subject.

It would therefore seem that we have another possible example of what we might call Hosea's embryonic covenant theology found elsewhere in the use of *berit* in Hosea 6:7, 8:1, which indicates the important part Hosea played in the development of Hebrew theology.

If this is so, then the circumstances of Hosea's marriage served as the impetus for the idea that Yahweh's election of Israel was not unconditional, but could be terminated. We shall shortly argue that this idea was taken up by later theologians intent on warning southern Judah that the same fate which had swept away her northern neighbour could engulf her too.

Finally, we should note that, despite the prophets' vivid language, there is little evidence from their charges (apart from the interpolation in Hosea 4:2) that the prophets spoke against the background of a general breakdown of law and order. This is confirmed by the picture Amos presents of a prosperous people confident that their prosperity resulted from their faithfulness to Yahweh, seen not only in their excessive religious zeal but also, we must assume, in outwardly ensuring the maintenance of an orderly society. Hence we find the business community constrained by the requirement to keep the Sabbath law (Amos 8:4-6).

Rather it was what was going on under the surface which indicated how rotten society was—the oppression of those who could not protect themselves and the manipulation of that justice that should have been theirs. This explains the eighth-century prophets' concentration on issues of humaneness and righteousness and their condemnation of current religious practice.

Of course, the nature of their society should have been obvious enough (Amos 3:9-10), but it is all too easy for those with power to overlook the conditions of the powerless where, despite an ordered and prosperous economy, the gap between rich and poor continues to widen, for which there is no legal redress. Tragically, the prophets' message remains as relevant today as it was in their own times.

CHAPTER 3

Covenant Theology

i. Hezekiah's Reform

In 721 the unthinkable happened. Both Hebrew kingdoms had been encouraged by the promise to Abraham fulfilled in David to see themselves as special in Yahweh's plans for his world. In spite of prophetic warnings that he could no longer be indifferent to the state of their society, they had nonetheless every reason to think their future was assured. Had they not been elected by him as his chosen people? But after years of turmoil as the expanding Assyrian empire moved westwards, and in which both kingdoms were forced to pay tribute as vassals, in 724 the northern kingdom revolted and, after a three-year war, fell to Assyria. Her leading citizens were deported and foreigners installed in their place. From that time on, the kingdom based on Samaria ceased to exist, becoming a province of that name within the Assyrian empire (2 Kings 17:1–6).

The southern kingdom of Judah, although threatened with conquest, was miraculously (2 Kings 19:25–26) enabled to continue as an independent vassal of Assyria under her king Hezekiah, whom those responsible for the Book of Kings single out above all others for their unqualified praise for the religious reforms he undertook:

> It was he who suppressed the shrines, smashed the sacred pillars, cut down every sacred pole, and broke up the bronze serpent that Moses had made, for up to that time the Israelites had been in the habit of burning sacrifices to it; they called it Nehushtan. He put his trust in the Lord God of Israel; there was nobody like

him among all the kings of Judah who succeeded him or among
those who had gone before him.

2 Kings 18:4–5

There can be little doubt that it was the shock of the obliteration of the
northern kingdom that forced theologians in Jerusalem to reassess Judah's
relationship with Yahweh. Clearly this was no longer guaranteed. Perhaps
drawing on Hosea, the covenant concept now emerged as an explanation
for what had occurred. And in the form of the suzerainty treaty which
had dominated the two kingdoms' political life for decades lay a ready
model for this new understanding of Israel's relationship with her God.

While under the treaty form the vassal was given independent
authority within his kingdom and also guaranteed the protection of
the suzerain from any enemy, in return the latter demanded the vassal's
absolute loyalty, so ruling out any independent foreign policy. In the same
way, theologians interpreted Yahweh as Israel's suzerain, guaranteeing her
protection but absolutely ruling out any possibility of her worshipping
any other deity. In their view, it was Israel's ambiguous attitude towards
Canaanite religion and her failure to give Yahweh her sole allegiance
which had resulted in the Assyrian conquest. No longer were Israel's
relations with her God seen only in terms of election. That election was
now recognised as conditional and able to be terminated.

It is at this point that a radical reinterpretation was introduced into
the Sinai narrative following Israel's new understanding of the nature of
her God. That narrative had been part of the original document of title
created in the early years of the Davidic monarchy. Now the covenant
concept was inserted into it and its breach and re-forming described.
In this way, southern Judah, which now assumes the mantle of Israel, is
given the necessary assurance that she is still Yahweh's elect, but reminded
that that election is not automatic come what may, but depends on her
unquestioned loyalty. She too could suffer Yahweh's final rejection. So
the covenant concept was introduced into the Exodus narrative of the
giving of the law at Sinai, but introduced in order to be broken and
re-established for the new Israel of the reforming king, Hezekiah.

The interpolations into the original Sinai narrative (Exodus 19–24)
are easily identifiable as, in contrast to the original text, they are all in

the plural form of address, indicating that they belong together as later additions.

The Decalogue (Exodus 20:1–17), which we shall consider in the next section, and the Book of the Covenant (Exodus 21:1–23:19) are now framed by a new preface (Exodus 19:3–8) which clearly sets out the covenant relationship between Yahweh and Israel:

> Moses went up to God, and the Lord called to him from the mountain and said, "This is what you are to say to the house of Jacob and tell the sons of Israel: You yourselves have seen what I did to Egypt, and how I have carried you on eagles' wings and brought you here to me. If only you will now listen to me and keep my covenant, then out of all peoples you will become my special possession; for the whole earth is mine. You will be to me a kingdom of priests, my holy nation. Those are the words you are to speak to the Israelites". Moses went down, and summoning the elders of the people he set before them all these commands which the Lord had laid on him. As one the people answered, "Whatever the Lord has said we will do".

The narrative then concludes with the covenant ceremony described in Exodus 24:3–8:

> Moses went and repeated to the people all the words of the Lord, all his laws. With one voice the whole people answered, "We will do everything the Lord has told us". Moses wrote down all the words of the Lord. Early in the morning he built an altar at the foot of the mountain, and erected twelve sacred pillars for the twelve tribes of Israel. He sent the young men of Israel and they sacrificed bulls to the Lord as whole-offerings and shared-offerings. Moses took half the blood and put it in basins, and the other half he flung against the altar. Then he took the Book of the Covenant and read it aloud for the people to hear. They said, "We shall obey, and do all that the Lord has said". Moses then took the blood and flung it over the people, saying, "This is the

blood of the covenant which the Lord has made with you on the
terms of this book".

This framework also includes Exodus 20:22–23, a preface to the laws of
the Book of the Covenant which highlights the prohibition of molten
images, a clear reference to the bull images of the northern kingdom:

> The Lord said to Moses, "Say this to the Israelites: You know
> now that I have spoken from heaven to you. You must not make
> gods of silver to be worshipped besides me, nor may you make
> yourselves gods of gold".

The story then continues in Exodus 32–34, the intervening chapters
Exodus 25–31 being a much later redaction of the Sinai narrative
following the exile. Moses is now pictured as ascending the mountain
to receive, as in any suzerainty agreement, two tablets of the law, one for
each party. There then follows the account of the making of the golden
calf, described as "your gods" (Exodus 32:4). When Moses descends from
the mountain and sees the calf, he breaks the tablets of the law as a sign
of the end of Yahweh's relationship with Israel. Finally, Moses receives the
gift of a second set of tablets with the laws of Exodus 34:11–26 inscribed
on them, signifying the restoration of the covenant relationship with
surviving Judah, now all that is left of the original Israel.

It is clear that the bull images are central to the revision of the Sinai
narrative. There can be no doubt that the author has in mind the bull
images which Jeroboam I, the first king of Israel, constructed for his
sanctuaries at Dan and Bethel (1 Kings 12:28–30). It may have been
that they were originally intended to act as pedestals for the invisible
Yahweh, like the ark in the temple at Jerusalem. However, as was noted
in the previous chapter, in the northern kingdom bull images came to be
worshipped in their own right (Hosea 8:5–6).

Earlier scholars were mistaken in arguing that the eighth-century
prophets were calling Israel back to a pre-existing covenant relationship.
Rather, it is as a result of the warnings contained in their preaching and
confirmed in the obliteration of the northern kingdom that theologians
in Jerusalem—forerunners of those later termed Deuteronomists because

of their association with the book of that name—introduced the covenant concept, thereby mistakenly limiting God's election of Israel. Such election could in their view be terminated, just as a political suzerain could terminate a vassal treaty.

It would seem that, as part of reaffirming that Yahweh was still Israel's God, Hosea's use of the derivation of Yahweh's name from the verb "to be", though now in a positive sense, was introduced into Exodus 3:14a. Whereas Hosea had threatened that Yahweh would be a "no I AM" to Israel, those southern theologians who introduced the covenant concept into the Sinai narrative asserted that, despite what had happened to the northern kingdom, Yahweh was still I AM in Jerusalem as long as they kept the covenant provisions.

For many years the laws of Exodus 34:11–26 were termed the Ritual Decalogue in contrast to the provisions of Exodus 20:1–17, termed the Ethical Decalogue, both being attributed to different sources behind the Pentateuch. This can no longer be maintained. In the first place, despite the late addition of Exodus 34:28, Exodus 34:11–26 is not a Decalogue, but contains more than ten provisions. Second, the provisions of Exodus 34:11–26 reflect the requirements of the new political situation occasioned by Hezekiah's radical reform, in which the king launched a full scale attack on Canaanite syncretism (2 Kings 18:4). Examination of the material shows it entirely fits such a milieu. That the authors of 2 Kings reduce Hezekiah's reform to one verse is due to their wish to boost the later reform of Josiah (2 Kings 23:1–25), which resulted in the Book of Deuteronomy and the accounts of the Davidic kings in the books of Samuel and Kings. Nonetheless, no other king has such praise lavished on him as does Hezekiah (2 Kings 18:5).

As the new covenant relationship requires, the laws of Exodus 34:11–26 warn against fraternising with the Canaanites. So they forbid the making of a covenant with them (v. 12), order the destruction of their altars and cult apparatus (v. 13), command the worship of Yahweh alone (vv. 14–15), and counsel against intermarriage of Israelite men with the daughters of the indigenous population (v. 16). As we shall see, these provisions will be further developed as a result of Josiah's reform (Deuteronomy 7).

Exodus 34:17 goes on to prohibit the making of a molten god, in the context obviously referring back to the golden calf of Exodus 32, and explains why Hezekiah destroyed the bronze serpent Nehushtan, even though its creation was attributed to no less a person than Moses himself (2 Kings 18:4). Finally, there follows in Exodus 34:22–24 a repeat of the festal calendar of Exodus 23:14–17 which, with its reference to the absence of "covetous neighbours", now clearly requires the centralisation of the three main festivals at Jerusalem. That some kind of centralisation of worship took place is confirmed by the Assyrian Rabshakeh's speech in 2 Kings 18:22.

It seems that Hezekiah's reform did not long outlast his reign, for under his successor Manasseh syncretism appears to have flourished. It was left to his successor Josiah to throw off the Assyrian yoke and introduce an even more far-reaching reform.

ii. The Decalogue

The study of the Decalogue is fraught with controversy. In slightly different versions it is found in Exodus 20 and Deuteronomy 5 and in both cases it acts as a prologue to subsequent laws, thereby giving them proper authority.

The Decalogue itself seems to have been formed from two components. The first five "religious" commandments demand the exclusive worship of the imageless Yahweh, whose name is not to be used for any improper purpose, the keeping of the Sabbath, and ensuring that parents are to be honoured. The remaining five commandments seem to reflect an earlier criminal law code alluded to in Hosea 4:2 and later Jeremiah 7:9 and reflected in the distinction between criminal and civil offences seen in the provisions of the Book of the Covenant.

It seems most likely that the first five commandments were formed and attached to the criminal law code at the same time as the covenant concept entered Israel's theology. For this reason, many scholars have in fact argued that the Decalogue was the creation of the Deuteronomists, exponents of a classical covenant theology. But in my view, it seems more probable to locate the origin of the Decalogue in Hezekiah's reform, when the covenant idea first entered Israel's theology and was inserted into the Exodus narrative.

First, the Deuteronomic version of the Decalogue makes subtle changes to the Exodus version in accordance with Deuteronomic theology, which we will examine later. Second, Deuteronomy's variation of the Exodus narrative by insisting that the Decalogue alone was written on the second set of tablets is designed to suppress the laws of Exodus 34:11–26 in favour of the new, all-important Deuteronomic legislation reflecting the much more far-reaching reform of Josiah, to which the Decalogue acts as a legitimising prologue, as it did to the Book of the Covenant.

The reason that the ancient criminal law code probably goes back to the time of David and was attached to the first five commandments is that it protected the person of each individual member of what is now seen as the covenant community. Each member was of individual concern to Yahweh. Where a breach of these criminal laws occurred, the community would, as in the past, continue to take action to punish the offender by inflicting the death penalty through stoning.

Clearly, the overriding concern of the Decalogue is to ensure Israel's exclusive relationship with Yahweh. But there is no thought of monotheism behind the first commandment. It does not seek to repudiate the existence of other gods, but to prevent Israel from having anything to do with them, even ruling out a consort for Yahweh. Further, the second commandment ruled that Yahweh's cult should be imageless, an overriding concern of Hezekiah's reform. Nor was his name to be used for improper purposes. It is not blasphemy that is envisaged here, for the Israelites believed that if a man cursed God, then God would automatically strike him dead: it was the quickest way to commit suicide, which was Job's wife's advice to her afflicted husband (Job 2:9). Rather, the commandment sought to prevent God's name being abused by being used for magical purposes. The Sabbath had long been observed in Israel: it distinguished her from her neighbours and was part of her special relationship with Yahweh. Probably the fifth commandment also had a religious basis, namely that by submitting to their authority, children had no choice but to accept their parents' faith. Those born into Israel were to remain in Israel for life.

There now follows the five requirements of the ancient criminal law code now seen as part of covenant law, though from David's time part of Israel's legal practice. The commandment on murder speaks for itself. But there is no thought here of pacifism, the abolition of capital punishment or vegetarianism. Israel was constantly at war, punished by execution and ate meat.

Adultery was limited to sexual intercourse with a married or betrothed woman. It had nothing to do with sexual ethics, but was designed to ensure that the husband might be certain that his wife's children were his own. The ancient rite in Numbers 5:11–31 appears to be a method of assessing paternity.

The prohibition of theft refers to man theft, which was a crime carrying the death penalty (Exodus 21:16; Deuteronomy 24:7), rather than theft of property which, as we have seen earlier, resulted in a civil action for damages (Exodus 22:1–4). The law sought to prevent the sale of an Israelite outside the community, which for all practical purposes was as effective as murder. This is what happened to Joseph (Genesis 17). Indeed, in Deuteronomy 24:7, the man-thief is described in Hebrew as "the stealer of life". There was always the temptation of selling a fellow-countryman as a slave to foreign invaders. Even after the return from exile, Nehemiah had to take action on this very issue (Nehemiah 5:8).

While the ninth commandment is concerned with the giving of false evidence in court, it was probably limited to criminal cases in which the accused might wrongfully suffer the death penalty through perjury (Deuteronomy 19:16–21). The classic example of this crime is the case of Naboth (1 Kings 21).

In all probability, the tenth commandment was originally in a similar short form to its four predecessors and simply forbad seizure of a house. The concern of this injunction was not the house itself, but the effect of dispossession. This deprived the owner of his status as an elder in the community and therefore his right to play his part in the community's affairs, including the administration of justice. He in effect became a non-person. But once the elders were replaced by professional judges under Jehoshaphat's earlier reform (2 Chronicles 19:5–11), the commandment would have lost its original purpose and, by the time of Hezekiah, become redundant. This explains why the compiler of the Decalogue has spiritualised the original injunction, "covet" being substituted for a word for seizing, and then has added all other property which an Israelite might have obtained by agreement, purchase or gain. The commandment may have become redundant as far as the criminal law was concerned, but it still served a moral purpose, as Micah 2:2 indicates.

The importance of Hezekiah's reform cannot be exaggerated. The radical reinterpretation of Israel's original document of title by the insertion of the covenant concept, the Decalogue and the narrative of the destruction of the tablets of the law and their replacement not only provided an explanation for the loss of the northern kingdom, but would in time also serve as the model for the Deuteronomic explanation of Israel's conquest by the Babylonians and her subsequent exile. To that we must now turn.

CHAPTER 4

Strengthening Covenant Theology

i. Josiah's Reform

During Manasseh's long reign the covenant established by Hezekiah's reform was systematically broken. After his death (642) and the brief reign of his son Amon (642–640), it was left to his grandson Josiah to introduce an even more far-reaching reform (622) inspired by the finding of "the scroll of the law" in the temple (2 Kings 22). This discovery led to a strengthening of covenant theology, resulting not in a further redaction of the Exodus narrative but in an entirely new work, Deuteronomy. This new work (Deuteronomy 4:44–26, 28) was, after the exile in Babylon, enlarged (Deuteronomy 1–4:43, 27, 29–30) and used to introduce an account of Israel's history from entry into the land of Canaan to her exile in Babylon (Joshua–2 Kings), the kings of both the northern and southern kingdoms being judged retrospectively in the light of Deuteronomic legal requirements.

The most far-reaching element of Josiah's reform was the centralisation of all worship in a purified temple at Jerusalem, with the consequent wholesale destruction of all other sanctuaries (2 Kings 23). Deuteronomy 12:2–7, which requires the demolition of all sanctuaries and their cult apparatus and the worship of Yahweh at "the place which the Lord your God will choose out of all your tribes to receive his name that it may dwell there", certainly reflects Josiah's centralisation policy. This indicates that the original Book of Deuteronomy must have been composed in its wake and designed to enforce its requirements in the hope that the southern kingdom might not endure the same disaster as had befallen her northern neighbour.

That Josiah was able to institute his reform was due to the rapid decline of the Assyrian empire. Indeed, his reform was an attempt to gain independence for Israel. He even journeyed to the territory of the old northern kingdom with the clear intention of restoring the united kingdom of David and Solomon (2 Kings 23:15–20). But such freedom as he obtained was short-lived.

When the Egyptian Pharaoh Necho marched his army up Israel's coastal plain to support Assyria in the face of rising Babylonian power, Josiah, attempting to stop him, was killed at the Battle of Megiddo (609) and with his death (2 Kings 23:29) died any hope of an independent Israel.

There has been no agreement over the identity of the scroll "discovered" in the temple and described in 2 Kings 23:2 as "the scroll of the covenant". Since the original Book of Deuteronomy reflects Josiah's reform, it seems probable that this discovered scroll was the redacted document of title following Hezekiah's reform, which introduced the covenant concept based on the political suzerainty treaty as an explanation of Israel's relationship with her God (Exodus 19–24, 32–34). This must have inspired Josiah to implement his more radical reform.

Indeed, the introduction to the laws of Deuteronomy relies on the redacted Exodus Sinai narrative, which it transforms for its own theological purpose (Deuteronomy 5–11). But because the later authors of Deuteronomy and its associated work Joshua–2 Kings undoubtedly suppressed the importance of the earlier reform of Hezekiah in order to emphasise Josiah's more sweeping one, the nature of the scroll would not have been spelt out, though its description clearly indicates that it was concerned with covenant theology.

In contrast to the Exodus narrative, the authors of Deuteronomy introduced the two tablets of the law immediately after the giving of the Decalogue (Deuteronomy 5:22), whereas in the earlier account they do not appear until after the Book of the Covenant has been mediated to Moses. Further, they reconstructed the account of their replacement. So, in Deuteronomy 9:1–10:11, after the incident of the golden calf and the breaking of the first set of tablets of the law, they assert that it was the Decalogue which was again written on the second set of tablets. In this way they successively suppressed both the Book of the Covenant and the laws of Exodus 34:11-26, the core of Hezekiah's reform. For the Deuteronomists, the Decalogue from which the laws of Deuteronomy 12-26 are pictured as deduced is the sole covenant law, obedience to which determines Israel's relationship with her God and her future presence in the land he had chosen to give her. Whether or not "the scroll" was the redacted document of title (Exodus 19-24, 32-34) following Hezekiah's reform, certainly the author of Deuteronomy deliberately rewrote the earlier Sinai narrative, of which he must have been fully aware, for his new work. Even the mountain where Moses received the Decalogue is renamed Horeb.

ii. Deuteronomy

The Deuteronomists had no doubt that it was apostasy that had led to the northern kingdom's rejection by her suzerain Yahweh. Their fear is that the surviving southern kingdom might suffer the same fate. They saw the cause of apostasy in the fact that the Canaanites had not been entirely eliminated when the Hebrews entered the land. Had this happened they would not have been tempted to adopt their heathen practices. This is clearly seen in the laws on warfare, where, in contrast to the treatment to be meted out to the cities of foreign nations, the inhabitants of the Canaanite cities are to be totally annihilated:

> In the towns of these nations whose land the Lord your God is giving you as your holding, you must not leave a soul alive. As the Lord your God commanded you, you must destroy them under solemn ban—Hittites, Amorites, Canaanites, Perizzites, Hivites, Jebusites—so that they may not teach you to imitate their abominable practices they have carried on for their gods, and so cause you to sin against the Lord your God.
>
> *Deuteronomy 20:16-18*

This is a decidedly ahistorical assessment of the past for, as we have seen, the nation built up by David and Solomon was a combination of those who had entered the land from outside as well as members of the indigenous population, many of whose religious ideas were adopted for Yahweh. Thanks to Canaanite religion, the Hebrews were able to understand their God as not only one who revealed himself in historical events, but also as the God who governed nature and fertility, the Lord of creation itself. It is true that there were some puritan sects among the Israelites who rejected everything Canaanite, the Nazarites (Amos 2) and Rechabites (Jeremiah 35), but as the Psalter with its considerable debt to Canaanite worship indicates, they were the exception. So, for instance, Psalm 29 was originally a Canaanite psalm, but now has Baal's name crossed out and Yahweh's substituted.

Regarding other aspects of the Deuteronomic reform, nothing in the laws alters my understanding of the distinction between criminal and civil offences identified in the so-called Book of the Covenant. Indeed, the Deuteronomic laws have almost no concern with civil offences apart from laying down the amount of damages to be paid by a husband for falsely accusing his wife of loss of virginity before marriage (Deuteronomy 22:19) and standardising damages payable for the seduction of a virgin (Deuteronomy 22:28-29).

While there are a number of criminal law enactments, the most striking characteristic of the Deuteronomic corpus is the amount of legislation requiring the exercise of charity, though the provisions enjoining this would have been impossible to enforce through the courts.

So, for instance, while Deuteronomy reiterates the law of the release of the Hebrew slave after six years' service, found in Exodus 21:2-6, the amendment in Deuteronomy 15:13-14 requires that the master must amply provide for the slave to start out on his new life:

> And when you set him free, do not let him go empty-handed.
> Give to him lavishly from your flock, from your threshing floor
> and your winepress. Be generous to him, as the Lord your God
> has blessed you.

As debt was the chief cause of slavery, there are lengthy provisions enacting the release of debts of fellow Israelites but not foreigners:

> At the end of every seventh year you must make a remission of debts. This is how it is to be made: everyone who holds a pledge shall return the pledge of the person indebted to him. He must not press a fellow-countryman for repayment, for the Lord's year of remission has been declared. You may press foreigners; but if it is a fellow-countryman that holds anything of yours, you must renounce all claim on it.
>
> *Deuteronomy 15:1–3*

The type of debt here envisaged involved a loan in return for the pledge of a person as security, who on failure to repay the loan was taken by the creditor, who used his services as compensation. Thus if a loan had not been paid back by the year of release, it could not subsequently be recovered and anyone who had been seized as pledge would have been released. Further, the Deuteronomic law enjoined that, even if the year of release was imminent, Israelites were still to lend generously to those in need (Deuteronomy 15:9–11). Deuteronomy 23:19–20 also repeats the provision of the Book of the Covenant (Exodus 22:25) that loans to fellow Israelites are to be free of interest.

Further, there are a number of laws designed to alleviate poverty (Deuteronomy 24:6, 12–15) and to make provision for the widow, orphan and resident alien:

> You must not deprive aliens and the fatherless of justice or take a widow's cloak in pledge. Bear in mind that you were slaves in Egypt and the Lord your God redeemed you from there; that is why I command you to do this. When you reap the harvest in your field and overlook a sheaf, do not go back to pick it up; it is to be left for the alien, the fatherless, and the widow, so that the Lord your God may bless you in all that you undertake. When you beat your olive trees, do not strip them afterwards; what is left is for the alien, the fatherless and the widow. When you gather the grapes from your vineyard, do not glean afterwards; what is left

is for the alien, the fatherless, and the widow. Keep in mind that
you were slaves in Egypt; that is why I command you to do this.

Deuteronomy 24:17–22

Appeal for the exercise of charity is based on Yahweh's own generosity
towards Israel in delivering her from slavery in Egypt. This is also the
explanation now offered for keeping the Sabbath commandment set out
in an extension to the Decalogue (Deuteronomy 5:12–15). The fact that
Israel had once been slaves not only justifies the demand that her own
slaves should be released from routine work on the Sabbath, but explains
why it was instituted in the first place. The Deuteronomists, in the light
of Josiah's bid for independence, were probably making a political point.
While slavery in Egypt would have meant no break in daily routine work,
Yahweh's deliverance had brought them the freedom to order their own
working life. While he had every right to regulate Istrael's work pattern
as her suzerain, he did so in such a way that the Sabbath became yet a
further instance of his grace.

As a result of the Deuteronomic reform itself, a new class of
dependents entered Israelite society. These were the country Levites
who would have been dispossessed of their livelihood following Josiah's
centralisation of all worship at Jerusalem. Though the Deuteronomic
legislation (Deuteronomy 18:6–8) provided that these disposed clergy
were entitled to come to Jerusalem and take part in worship there and
so secure their livelihood, the Jerusalem priesthood prevented this (2
Kings 23:9). Consequently, alongside the widow, orphan and resident
alien, they became entitled to charitable support:

Also, the Levites who live in your settlements must not suffer
neglect at your hands, for they have no holding of ancestral land
among you. At the end of every third year you are to bring out all the
tithe of your produce for that year and leave it in your settlements
so that the Levites, who have no holding of ancestral land among
you, and the aliens, orphans, and widows in your settlements may
come and have plenty to eat. If you do this the Lord your God will
bless you in everything to which you set your hand.

Deuteronomy 14:27–29

Israel's law recognised that it was in the interests of all that no one should be in distress. For widespread poverty can only lead to growing discontent and eventually to conflict and violence. Hebrew law was designed to prevent this.

Deuteronomy even extended its laws on charity to include travellers, who were expressly permitted to sustain themselves from the crops through which they passed on their journey (cf. Matthew 12:1), but were forbidden to take anything away with them:

> When you go into another man's vineyard, you may eat as many grapes as you wish to satisfy your hunger, but you may not put any into your basket. When you go into another man's standing grain, you may pluck ears to rub in your hands, but you may not put a sickle to the standing crop.
>
> *Deuteronomy 23:24-25*

The Deuteronomic laws on animals have long been recognised for their remarkable humanitarianism:

> You are not to muzzle an ox while it is treading out the grain.
>
> *Deuteronomy 25:4*

Further examples can be found in Deuteronomy 22:1-4, 6-7, 10.

And, like the Book of the Covenant, the laws also emphasise the importance of the reliability of the administration of justice:

> You must not pervert the course of justice or show favour or accept a bribe; for bribery makes the wise person blind and the just person give a crooked answer.
>
> *Deuteronomy 16:19*

One notable innovation of the Deuteronomists was to make women equally liable as men under the law (Deuteronomy 12:12, 18; 16:11, 14; 29:11, 18). Before the reform only men had full legal responsibility. So, in the case of the crime of adultery in what is clearly new legislation, it is specifically spelt out that the offending woman as well as the man is to be executed:

> When a man is discovered lying with a married woman, both are to be put to death, the woman as well as the man who lay with her: you must purge Israel of this wickedness.
>
> *Deuteronomy 22:22*

Similarly, the warning against marrying sons to Canaanite daughters in Exodus 34:16 is now extended to a prohibition which includes not only sons marrying Canaanites, but daughters too:

> You must not intermarry with them, giving your daughters to their sons or taking their daughters for your sons, because if you do, they will draw your children away from the Lord to serve other gods.
>
> *Deuteronomy 7:3–4*

And the positioning of the neighbour's wife instead of the neighbour's house at the head of the items that could be coveted in the tenth commandment again reflects the Deuteronomists' concern for women (Deuteronomy 5:21).

But whatever additions or amendments were made to the criminal or civil law or the laws of humaneness and righteousness, the overriding preoccupation of the Deuteronomic reform remained apostasy. This is what had brought the northern kingdom to her knees. Each member of the covenant community had a duty to root out all offenders and have them exterminated, however close they were, as a deterrent to others who might similarly be tempted:

> If your brother, your father's son or your mother's son, or your son or daughter, your beloved wife, or your dearest friend should entice you secretly to go and serve other gods—gods of whom neither you nor your fathers have had experience, gods of the people round about you, near or far, at one end of the land or the other—then you must not consent or listen. Show none of

them mercy, neither spare nor shield them; you are to put them
to death, your own hand being the first to be raised against them,
and then all the people are to follow. Stone them to death, because
they tried to lead you astray from the Lord your God who brought
you out of Egypt, out of that land where you were slaves. All Israel
when they hear of it will be afraid; never again will anything as
wicked as this be done among you.

Deuteronomy 13:6–11

Examination of the phrase "jealous God" indicates that it is only used
where Yahweh sees his exclusive covenant relationship with Israel
threatened by her apostasy in acknowledging other gods (Exodus 20:5;
Deuteronomy 4:24, 5:9, 6:15). God is jealous for that relationship. He has
of his grace chosen Israel as his elect community, through whom he wills
to manifest his nature to all nations (Genesis 12:3). Without Israel, how
will other peoples ever know that nature? And that nature is reflected
in his law, the complete expression of his will for his people and so for
humankind in general.

It is for this reason that the authors of Deuteronomy warn that once
Israel enjoys the affluence of Canaan, she should not forget her God. God
had willed Israel's prosperity and had brought her to the land of milk
and honey in which she is to luxuriate. But Deuteronomy expresses the
fear that once Israel has become self-sufficient, she might be tempted to
abandon her God as no longer necessary for her survival:

See that you do not forget the Lord your God by failing to keep
his commandments, laws, and statutes which I give you this day.
When you have plenty to eat and live in fine houses of your own
building, when your herds and flocks, your silver and gold, and
all your possessions increase, do not become proud and forget
the Lord your God who brought you out of Egypt, out of the
land of slavery.

Deuteronomy 8:11–14

The consequences of failure could only be judgment.

iii. Judgment

Having defeated Egypt at the Battle of Carchemish (605), it was only a matter of time before the Babylonians conquered Jerusalem (598) and led her king Jehoiachin and more important citizens into exile in Babylon (2 Kings 24:10–17). Further rebellion under his successor Zedekiah, the last Davidic king, led Babylon to attack again and this time the temple, the meeting place of God and his people, was destroyed and Jerusalem razed to the ground, the king and further citizens being taken into exile (2 Kings 25:1–21). Israel now became a province of Babylon ruled by a Governor Gedaliah, a Babylonian appointee (2 Kings 25:22). The enormity of the disaster cannot be exaggerated:

> How deserted lies the city,
> once thronging with people!
> Once great among nations,
> now become a widow;
> once queen among provinces,
> now put to forced labour!
>
> *Lamentations 1:1*

This was not all: according to Israel's theologians, it was not Babylonian military prowess which had brought these catastrophic events upon Israel, but her own God. He alone had secured her defeat and devastation, thereby indicating that his relationship with her was at an end. The jealous God had acted and the threat contained in the covenant had been executed. No longer was Yahweh prepared to call his own those who had so openly flouted the principles of his divine nature. Israel had in effect judged herself and had no one but herself to blame for the horrific situation in which she found herself. Now even the assurance of the presence of God given to Israel through the temple had been terminated. What hope was there for the future?

CHAPTER 5

Restoration and Renewal

i. The Deuteronomists

The Deuteronomists were the first group of theologians faced with the task of trying to come to terms with God's apparent absolute judgment on Israel. Their difficulty was that God had done what they themselves believed he would do, broken the covenant relationship with his chosen people. Was there any way back?

Between 560 and 540, they published their work Deuteronomy–2 Kings, giving Deuteronomy itself a new introductory prologue Deuteronomy 1–4:43 and setting out the history of Israel from entry into Canaan to the exile in accordance with their theological understanding of how those who had led the two kingdoms had conformed to their law. There was no question that God had acted unjustly, nor could he be blamed if his patience had finally run out. Israel had had ample warning and had chosen to ignore God's claims in spite of all he had done for her. She had broken the exclusive covenant relationship inaugurated by Moses on Mount Horeb and for her apostasy had been condemned.

The publication of the Deuteronomists' work was probably inspired by the release of the exiled Jehoiachin from prison in Babylon in 561 (2 Kings 25:27), for this is the last event recorded in their "history". Undoubtedly, the king's release would have caused a wave of excitement to pass throughout Judaism, both in Babylon and Jerusalem. Was this the prelude to another mighty act of Israel's God whereby he would deliver his people from oppression so that they might again enjoy their unique relationship with him in the land he had chosen for them?

Both in their preface to the Book of Deuteronomy and in their history work, the Deuteronomists let drop that, despite the horror of the destruction of Jerusalem and Israel's exile in a heathen land, somewhat illogically they have not entirely given up all hope in a future for Israel with her God. They might yet turn and find him:

> The Lord will scatter you among the peoples, and you will be left few in number among the nations to which the Lord will lead you. There you will serve gods made by human hands out of wood and stone, gods that can neither see nor hear, eat nor smell. But should you from there seek the Lord your God, you will find him, if it is with all your heart and soul that you search. When you are in distress and all those things happen to you, you will in days to come turn back to the Lord your God and obey him. The Lord your God is a merciful God; he will never fail you or destroy you; he will not forget the covenant with your forefathers which he guaranteed by oath.
>
> *Deuteronomy 4:27–31*

Similarly, at the dedication of the temple, Solomon anticipates a possible exile, and Israel's repentance, praying that Yahweh will forgive them (1 Kings 8:46–53). But it is by a radical reinterpretation of an injunction in the original Book of Deuteronomy that the Deuteronomists assert that God himself will ensure Israel's obedience.

In Deuteronomy 10:16, the authors of Deuteronomy commanded the people to "circumcise their hearts". Two things need to be noted. First, for the Hebrews, the heart was not the seat of the emotions but of the intellect, the will. And second, before the exile, circumcision was not specifically linked to Israel's religion but was performed, as widely elsewhere, as an initiation into marriage (Genesis 34). So, in using circumcision metaphorically, the Deuteronomists are arguing that just as an uncircumcised ear does not listen (Jeremiah 6:10) and uncircumcised lips cannot speak (Exodus 6:12, 30), so an uncircumcised heart lacks steadfastness of will. If Israel is to avoid Yahweh's rejection she must undergo such a radical change of heart that it could only be described by comparison with the physical act of circumcision.

But in contrast Deuteronomy 30:6 records:

> The Lord your God will circumcise your hearts and the hearts of
> your descendants, so that you will love him with all your heart
> and soul and you will live.

This is part of a late insertion into the Book of Deuteronomy (29:2–30:20),
for it presupposes that the covenant relationship has been terminated and
that the curses laid down for its breach (27–28) have fallen on disobedient
Israel. Her land lies desolate and her leading citizens have been led into
exile. Yet the Deuteronomists offer scattered Israel hope. Even now she
may yet again know God's grace. Through repentance and submitting to
his law, Israel can yet again enjoy a future far more glorious than anything
hitherto envisaged. All this would be worked out in God's own time,
of which Jehoiachin's release would have been interpreted as a sign. In
this way the Deuteronomists sought to dissuade from apostasy a totally
bewildered people whose whole theological basis had suddenly collapsed.
Despite appearances to the contrary, by holding fast to Yahweh, they can
yet have a future.

But would there be any guarantee things might not end up in the same
way? How could Israel's obedience be guaranteed? As Deuteronomy 29:4
puts it:

> But to this day the Lord has not given you a mind to understand
> or eyes to see or ears to hear.

That is the significance of Deuteronomy 30:6. In some mysterious way,
Yahweh himself would do what he had hitherto sought his people to do
for themselves and which they had blatantly been unable to carry out:
he himself would circumcise their hearts and so enable his covenant to
be kept. He would give to his constantly rebellious people the will to love
him. It is a breathtaking promise to a people utterly defeated. It would
be left to other theologians to work out how this could be achieved,
which would in the end mean abandoning the suzerainty treaty model
for understanding the nature of Israel's God. So however dark things

appeared to be, and in the face of their own theology, the Deuteronomists still saw a future for the chosen people.

That future would though still depend on Israel's obedience to the law as set out in Deuteronomy, now seen as the complete expression of Yahweh's will. If ever again she crossed the Jordan and entered Canaan, faithfulness to that law provided the means whereby Israel could secure her future in the land which Yahweh willed to give her. Consequently, for the Deuteronomists the law remained a benefit and not a burden:

> What great nation has a god close at hand as the Lord our God is
> close to us whenever we call to him? What great nation is there
> whose statutes and laws are so just, as is all this code of laws which
> I am setting before you today?
>
> *Deuteronomy 4:7-8*

ii. Jeremiah

Jeremiah prophesied for forty years, starting before Josiah implemented his reform (627) and continuing until, following the assassination of Gedaliah (Jeremiah 41:18), his friends for his own safety took him to Egypt, where we must assume he died (Jeremiah 43:4-7). His prophecies thus covered the period of the five last Davidic kings.

As now presented, the Book of Jeremiah has been so heavily edited by the Deuteronomists that it is in effect part of their corpus. This results in it covering a period much longer than the prophet's life, much of the material reflecting the theology of the Deuteronomists working in the exilic period (560-540) and developing their ideas even further. Nonetheless, as opposed to the narrative, prose sayings and sermons, the oracles themselves probably reflect the prophet's own words and even in composing their own material the Deuteronomists would have relied on Jeremiah's prophecy.

Some of the early chapters of Jeremiah may date from before Josiah's reform (Jeremiah 2-3). It is clear that, in contrast to his son, he admired that king (Jeremiah 22:13–17). Although in its present form the famous temple sermon preached in 609 at the beginning of Jehoiakim's reign (Jeremiah 26:1) is a Deuteronomic composition, something of Jeremiah's own message can be discerned.

In the sermon, Jeremiah unhesitatingly condemns Israel, not only for her attitude to the defenceless in her society as well as apostasy, but also for what appear to be breaches of the commandments of the Decalogue. The assumption that, because Israel has the temple Yahweh must be present in it, is rejected, the destruction of the shrine at Shiloh being cited as proof that God can destroy his own sanctuary if he so chooses. While Shiloh had been an important shrine at the time of Saul, archaeology has shown that reference is here being made to a recent sacking by the Babylonians:

> You keep saying, "This place is the temple of the Lord, the temple of the Lord, the temple of the Lord!" This slogan of yours is a lie; put no trust in it. If you amend your ways and your deeds, deal fairly with one another, cease to oppress the alien, the fatherless, and the widow, if you shed no innocent blood in this place and do not run after other gods to your own ruin, then I shall let you live in this place, in the land which long ago I gave to your forefathers for all time. You gain nothing by putting your trust in this lie. You steal, you murder, you commit adultery and perjury, you burn sacrifices to Baal, and you run after other gods whom you have not known … Go to my shrine at Shiloh, which once I made a dwelling for my name, and see what I did to it because of the wickedness of my people Israel.
>
> *Jeremiah 7:4–9, 12*

But the overall message that the Deuteronomic editors wanted to purvey in their use of the life and prophecies of Jeremiah was one of hope that, despite the inevitable destruction that Israel's own God was bringing upon his people, heralded by the prophet, there was yet a future which God alone would ensure. Indeed, the prophet appears himself to have had hope in Israel's place in the land, for when Jerusalem was being besieged

by the Babylonians before the second conquest, he deliberately purchased
a field at Anathoth, his birthplace (Jeremiah 32).

The Deuteronomists' hope in the future is spelt out in Jeremiah 31,
another passage composed in their characteristic style. First, they reject
a popular proverb:

> In those days it will no longer be said,
> "Parents have eaten sour grapes
> and the children's teeth are set on edge";
> for everyone will die from his own wrong-doing;
> he who eats sour grapes will find his teeth set on edge.
>
> *Jeremiah 31:29–30*

Here they are citing their own criminal law provision:

> Parents are not to be put to death for their children, nor children
> for their parents; each one may be put to death only for his own sin.
>
> *Deuteronomy 24:16*

Each generation is responsible for its own actions, which cannot affect a
subsequent generation. So, while Yahweh may condemn those who have
so blatantly rejected him, he can yet bless those who follow. And using
the same idea expressed in Deuteronomy 30:6, Yahweh spells out how
he will achieve this:

> The days are coming, says the Lord, when I shall establish a new
> covenant with the people of Israel and Judah. It will not be like
> the covenant I made with their forefathers when I took them by
> the hand to lead them out of Egypt, a covenant they broke, though
> I was patient with them, says the Lord. For this is the covenant I
> shall establish with the Israelites after those days, says the Lord: I
> shall set my law within them, writing it on their hearts; I shall be
> their God, and they will be my people. No longer need they teach
> one another, neighbour or brother to know the Lord; all of them,

high and low alike, will know me, says the Lord, for I shall forgive
their wrongdoing, and their sin I shall call to mind no more.

Jeremiah 31:31-34

By writing the law on Israel's heart, God will give them the will to keep
his covenant. The call of Jeremiah to "circumcise your hearts" (Jeremiah
4:4) will be effected by God himself with the result that their position
as his chosen people will no longer be under threat, but be assured. The
suzerainty treaty model is utterly rejected: in effect the Deuteronomists
are heralding a return to that grace theology which marked Israel's origins
and was set out in her document of title. It was left to others in the exilic
situation to develop their reassessment of Israel's relationship with her
God.

Finally, we may note that the parable of the two baskets of good and
bad figs confirms that the Deuteronomists recognised that the future of
Israel lay with the exiles (Jeremiah 24):

> These are the words of the Lord the God of Israel: I count the
> exiles of Judah whom I sent away from this place to the land of
> the Chaldaeans as good as these good figs. I shall look to their
> welfare, and restore them to this land; I shall build them up and
> not pull them down, plant them and not uproot them. I shall
> give them the wit to know me, for I am the Lord; they will be my
> people and I shall be their God, for they will come back to me
> wholeheartedly.

Jeremiah 24:5-7

No one was under any illusion that that would occur any time soon
(Jeremiah 28).

iii. Ezekiel

So it was in exile in Babylon that Israel's theologians were forced to reassess Israel's understanding of the nature of her relationship with her God. Once more, a radical change in her circumstances brought about by political events would determine her theology.

The first person to attempt to come to terms with the catastrophe of exile and the question of the future was the prophet Ezekiel, who had been taken to Babylon with the first deportees in 597. At first sight, the book that bears his name looks highly ordered. Yet like so much of the Hebrew scriptures, it has been subject to considerable editing, with some prophecies being made to conform to what had in fact occurred (Ezekiel 12; 23:36–49). So the book opens with a vision of Yahweh leaving Jerusalem for exile with his people in Babylon and ends with a vision of the restoration of the Jerusalem temple, with Yahweh again dwelling in Israel's midst (Ezekiel 40–48).

In his early ministry, Ezekiel concentrated on asserting that it was no good the first batch of exiles continuing to look back at Jerusalem in hope. Her fate was sealed. But once the temple had been destroyed and Jerusalem razed to the ground, the prophet had no alternative but to concentrate on the future. So in the prophecy setting out Israel's long history of disobedience, Ezekiel rejects any idea that there was any idyllic period in the past. Even in Egypt, before the exodus, they had rebelled against Yahweh. He should have destroyed them then:

> That day I swore with hand uplifted that I would bring them out
> of Egypt into the land I had sought out for them, a land flowing
> with milk and honey, the fairest of all lands. I told every one of
> them to cast away the loathsome things to which they looked
> up, and not to defile themselves with the idols of Egypt. I am the
> Lord your God, I said. But in rebellion against me they refused
> to listen, and not one of them cast away the loathsome things
> to which he looked up or forsook the idols of Egypt. I resolved
> to pour out my wrath and exhaust my anger on them in Egypt.
>
> *Ezekiel 20:6–8*

At each stage of Israel's history, God had every right to terminate his relationship with her. But to do so posed an insoluble dilemma. The destruction of Israel would have been interpreted by foreign nations as a defeat for Israel's God by their gods, and Yahweh would have been left without anyone to acknowledge him:

> But then I acted for the honour of my name, that it might not be profaned in the sight of the nations among whom Israel was living: I revealed myself to them by bringing Israel out of Egypt.
>
> *Ezekiel 20:9*

Both in the wilderness and in the land to which Yahweh had brought them, they continued their disobedience. Eventually their rebellion reached such a magnitude that God had to act. Faced without a people to worship him, Yahweh had no alternative but to restore his people to their land, a restoration which the nations will be forced to witness:

> You will know that I am the Lord, when I bring you home to the soil of Israel, to the land which I swore with uplifted hand to give your forefathers. There you will remember your past conduct and all the acts by which you defiled yourselves, and you will loathe yourselves for all the wickedness you have committed. You will know that I am the Lord, when I deal with you Israelites, not as your wicked ways and your vicious deeds deserve, but as the honour of my name demands. This is the word of the Lord God.
>
> *Ezekiel 20:42–44*

The restoration of Israel is not simply an act of undeserved grace towards Israel: it is also a vindication of Yahweh's power among the nations. They should be under no illusion as to who is in control of what happens in the world. Their gods are of no account when faced with Yahweh. It is he who is Lord both of creation and history.

Like Jeremiah (Jeremiah 31:29–30), whose prophecy he may well have known, Ezekiel rejects the proverb about sour grapes. Using the principle of criminal law to which this proverb alludes (Deuteronomy 24:16), Ezekiel reiterates that one generation cannot determine the fate of the next. Those responsible for the exile cannot decide the fate of their successors. That is in their own hands.

And again, as the Deuteronomists (Deuteronomy 30:6) and Jeremiah (Jeremiah 31:31–34) had asserted, it is Yahweh himself who will give this next generation the will to obey him:

> Say therefore: These are the words of the Lord God: I shall gather you from among the nations and bring you together from the countries where you have been dispersed, and I shall give the land of Israel to you. When they come there, they will abolish all the vile and abominable practices. I shall give them singleness of heart and put a new spirit in them; I shall remove the heart of stone from their bodies and give them a heart of flesh, so that they will conform to my statutes and keep my laws. They will be my people, and I shall be their God.
>
> *Ezekiel 11:17–20*

Ezekiel's theology is then dominated by his recognition of God's grace, beautifully brought out in his vision of the valley of dry bones (Ezekiel 37). The image here is not of resurrection but of re-creation. Israel is dead—like so many dry bones lying in a desert wadi after some Bedouin skirmish, bones picked dry by the vultures and bleached by the desert sun. The old order is at an end. There is a complete break. Then, of his own free will, God re-creates Israel and, as in the older creation story (Genesis 2), he clothes the bones with flesh and breathes into them the breath of life. So a new Israel is born, an Israel who has done nothing, undertaken nothing in return for her life, an Israel utterly dependent on God's grace for her existence:

> The Lord's hand was upon me, and he carried me out by his spirit and set me down in a plain that was full of bones. He made me pass among them in every direction. Countless in number and very dry, they covered the plain. He said to me, "O man, can these bones live?" I answered, "Only you, Lord God, know that." He said, "Prophesy over these bones; say: Dry bones, hear the word of the Lord. The Lord God says to these bones: I am going to put

breath into you, and you will live. I shall fasten sinews on you,
clothe you with flesh, cover you with skin, and give you breath,
and you will live. Then you will know that I am the Lord."

Ezekiel 37:1-6

Thus, from the wreck of the Babylonian conquest Ezekiel not only
proclaimed a future for his people, but also recovered for them the
essential nature of their relationship with their God, which reliance on
the form of the suzerainty treaty had distorted. In effect, they had trapped
God by the threat of the absolute breaking of the covenant. But God is
never trapped. He must, because of his nature, condemn utterly all that
is opposed to his holiness, even his chosen people. Yet beyond God's
judgment there is always a future. For God judges not to annihilate, but to
re-create. His anger is righteous and can only result in something positive.
When it came to the point, God could not let Israel go: nor would he
ever do so. And through her cult, the restoration of which is vividly
described by Ezekiel, her future was to be assured for all time. So God
again makes his presence known in his restored temple, from which, like
a river flowing from its doors, he floods the whole land with his blessing
(Ezekiel 40–48). As for Jerusalem herself, "for all time to come the city's
name will be 'The Lord is there'" (Ezekiel 48:35).

The Babylonian conquest had looked like the end: it was in reality the
restoration of a new and more wonderful relationship based on nothing
else than divine love. It is not too much to say that it is Ezekiel, rather
than Ezra, who deserves the title Father of Judaism. For it was through
his theological insight that post-exilic Israel found her future assured. He
realised the nature of the God with whom not just Israel, but all humankind,
has to deal. It was now up to the exiles to appropriate for themselves this
promised future. God could not do that for them. Men and women always
determine their own fate, though God never exhausts his love.

Though Ezekiel does not spell it out, at the centre of his theology is
the recognition that there is a necessary powerlessness in God's nature
(Ezekiel 20). For centuries God holds back from punishing his people
for their blatant apostasy, in effect held hostage by the other nations.
He recognises that to exercise judgment will in effect leave him without
a people, for the other nations will interpret Israel's defeat as due to

the powerlessness of her God in relation to their gods. In the end, he cannot afford to let Israel go. And as we shall discover, this apparent powerlessness is the costly price of love, which in the end constitutes God's very essence. Ironically, God's power is exercised in powerlessness.

iv. Deutero-Isaiah

The generation to whom Ezekiel prophesied was to die in exile without seeing the fulfilment of his prophecy. Inevitably this led to considerable anxiety. Perhaps after all he had been a false prophet, perhaps Babylonian gods were stronger than Yahweh, perhaps Israel's relationship with him had come to an end as covenant theology said it would. So those who against all the odds had remained faithful began to question his activity. What, if anything, was he doing on Israel's behalf?

It was in answer to such questioning that an unknown prophet of the exile wrote. He has become known as Deutero-Isaiah because his words have been attached to the prophecy of the eighth-century prophet Isaiah as chapters 40–55, though there has also been some editing of earlier material. His answer is a triumphant vindication of Israel's God, who even now was bringing into effect Israel's deliverance from her captors and inaugurating her return to her own land. Was it pure chance that the all-conquering Persian king Cyrus had appeared in the east to threaten Babylon?

> Who has raised up from the east
> one greeted by victory wherever he goes,
> making nations his subjects
> and overthrowing their kings?
> He scatters them with his sword like dust
> and with his bow like chaff driven before the wind;
> he puts them to flight and passes on unscathed,
> swifter than any traveller on foot.
> Whose work is this, who has brought it to pass?

Who has summoned the generations from the beginning?
I, the Lord, was with the first of them,
and I am with those who come after.

Isaiah 41:2–4

For those who had eyes to see, here was the hand of God stretched out again to save his people. Deutero-Isaiah thus reaffirms the prophecy of Ezekiel. Even now a second exodus is dawning. It will be quite different from the hasty flight from Egypt: instead, it will be a triumphant march across a transformed environment. Hills will be brought low and valleys exalted to make a pleasant plain across which to march. And it will be no secret affair, but will take place in full view of the nations, who will have to draw their own conclusions about the nature of Israel's God:

A voice cries:
"Clear a road through the wilderness for the Lord,
prepare a highway across the desert for our God.
Let every valley be raised,
every mountain and hill be brought low,
uneven ground be made smooth,
and steep places become level.
Then will the glory of the Lord be revealed
and all mankind together will see it.
The Lord himself has spoken."

Isaiah 40:3–5

There will be no need to stop at Sinai/Horeb for no obligations are to be imposed on Israel. By God's grace and God's grace alone she is to be restored to her own land in a relationship which nothing now can break. Deutero-Isaiah confirms this rejection of the pre-exilic threat theology based on the Sinai covenant by dramatically referring to Israel's three other ancient covenant traditions—all covenants of promise without obligation: the covenants with Noah (Genesis 8:21–22), Abraham (Genesis 17), and David (2 Samuel 7). So, of Noah he writes:

> For this to me is like the days of Noah;
> as I swore that the waters of Noah's flood
> should never again pour over the earth,
> so now I swear to you
> never again to be angry with you or to rebuke you.
> Though the mountains may move and the hills shake,
> my love will be immovable and never fail,
> and my covenant promising peace will not be shaken,
> says the Lord in his pity for you.
>
> *Isaiah 54:9–10*

Nothing could be more explicit. Similarly, appeal is made to the promise to Abraham:

> Consider Abraham your father
> and Sarah who gave you birth:
> when I called him he was but one;
> I blessed him and made him many.
> The Lord has comforted Zion,
> comforted all her ruined homes,
> turning her wilderness into an Eden,
> her arid plains into a garden of the Lord.
> Gladness and joy will be found in her,
> thanksgiving and melody.
>
> *Isaiah 51:2–3*

But the most significant of all is the use Deutero-Isaiah makes of the Davidic covenant tradition that David and his heirs would rule Israel for ever. Instead of looking for the restoration of the monarchy, the prophet transfers the promise to David to the nation. They now become the everlasting people who will exist for all time, come what may:

> Come to me and listen to my words,
> hear me and you will have life:

> I shall make an everlasting covenant with you
> to love you faithfully as I loved David.
>
> *Isaiah 55:3*

So for Deutero-Isaiah, Yahweh was even now bringing about the restoration of the elect people with all that that would entail: the only doubt was whether the exilic community would have sufficient faith to see his activity in the political events overtaking them, and so be able to claim his everlasting promise that he would be their God and they would be his people:

> I say to Cyrus, "You will be my shepherd
> to fulfil all my purpose,
> so that Jerusalem may be rebuilt
> and the foundations of the temple be laid."
>
> *Isaiah 44:28*

Deutero-Isaiah was the first Hebrew theologian explicitly to enumerate the doctrine of monotheism—that there is only one God. Previously, Israel had been charged to worship only one God, but had not only acknowledged the existence of other gods with whom she was supposed to have no dealings, but had even worshipped them. No doubt the fact that in Babylon the same claims were being made for the Babylonian god Marduk as for Israel's God Yahweh led Deutero-Isaiah to make his far-reaching assertion:

> Thus says the Lord, Israel's King,
> the Lord of Hosts, his Redeemer:
> I am the first and I am the last,
> and there is no god but me.
> Who is like me? Let him speak up;
> let him declare his proof and set it out for me:
> let him announce beforehand things to come,
> let him foretell what is yet to be.
> Take heart, have no fear,
> Did I not tell you this long ago?

> I foretold it, and you are my witnesses.
> Is there any god apart from me,
> any other deity? I know none!
>
> *Isaiah 44:6–8*

One of the immediate consequences of belief in monotheism was that the nations of the world could no longer be ignored. They must now have some relationship to Israel's God who, since he was the only God, must have created them. So, at a time of Israel's apparent total oblivion, Deutero-Isaiah proclaims Israel's role to the world:

> I shall appoint you a light to the nations
> so that my salvation may reach earth's farthest bounds.
>
> *Isaiah 49:6b*

The proclamation of the "gospel" of God's grace—which will be confirmed by his action in restoring his people from their exile—is now to be Israel's timeless mission to the world:

> And you in turn will summon nations you do not know,
> and nations that do not know you will hasten to you,
> because the Lord your God,
> Israel's Holy One, has made you glorious.
>
> *Isaiah 55:5*

But in the end the glorious future that Deutero-Isaiah proclaimed would only be achieved if there were still those who, against all the odds, had remained faithful to Yahweh in Babylon. In the face of, on the one hand, widespread apostasy in Babylon and, on the other, the multitude of heathen nations to whom the prophet argued Israel now had a responsibility, the future would depend on the faithfulness of a few. This explains the role of the suffering servant designated to ensure that future through his suffering on behalf of others (Isaiah 42:1–4; 49:1–6; 50:4–9; 52:13–53:12).

There has been much debate about the identity of the servant. In a work dominated by the exodus theme, the model is undoubtedly Moses, who in the story of the golden calf offered to suffer vicariously for his people:

> The next day Moses said to the people, "You have committed a great sin. Now I shall go up to the Lord; perhaps I may be able to secure pardon for your sin." When he went back to the Lord he said, "Oh, what a great sin this people has committed; they have made themselves gods of gold. Now if you will forgive them, forgive; but if not, blot out my name, I pray, from your book which you have written." The Lord answered Moses, "Whoever has sinned against me, him I shall block out from my book."
>
> *Exodus 32:30–33*

However, we must not confuse the model for the identity of the servant specifically described in the text as Israel. But the text shows that this servant is not the entire people of Israel in exile, but is the righteous within Israel as against all Israel. This explains how he can be both designated as Israel and yet have a ministry towards Israel:

> He said to me, "Israel, you are my servant
> through whom I shall win glory"
> And now the Lord has said to me:
> "It is too slight a task for you, as my servant,
> to restore the tribes of Jacob,
> to bring back the survivors of Israel."
>
> *Isaiah 49:3, 6a*

That salvation would not though be won by the exercise of power, but through the powerlessness of suffering and death:

> By his humiliation my servant will justify many;
> after his suffering he will see light and be satisfied;
> it is their guilt he bears.
> Therefore I shall allot him a portion with the great,
> and he will share the spoil with the mighty,
> because he exposed himself to death

and was reckoned among the transgressors,
for he bore the sin of many
and interceded for transgressors.

Isaiah 53:11–12

So Deutero-Isaiah appealed to his fellow Israelites in exile, now the second generation apparently forsaken by their God and of little consequence politically, to remain firm in their trust in Yahweh. It would be through their faithfulness in suffering and even death in a heathen land that not only would Israel be restored to her own land, but the whole world would come to know the nature of the one gracious God with whom humankind had to deal. But even as the unknown prophet of the exile spells out the blessing of Yahweh's unconditional grace, he asserts that it cannot be enjoyed without cost. Grace can never be cheap.

Israel then has an atoning role to play. It was through her that God and all humankind were to be at one. This is beautifully brought out in the metaphor of Israel as the priest nation, part of the post-exilic writings attached to Isaiah 1–55 and known by scholars as Trito-Isaiah (Isaiah 56–66):

Foreigners will serve as shepherds of your flocks,
aliens will till your land and tend your vines,
but you will be called priests of the Lord
and be named ministers of our God.
You will enjoy the wealth of nations
And succeed to their riches.

Isaiah 61:5–6

Just as in ancient Israel the priests, who were without any property, secured their livelihood from the laity who tilled the land, so now Israel, as the priest-nation to the world, is to live off the foreign nations pictured as the laity doing all the manual work. Israel though is not simply to luxuriate in her rich idleness: she has a specific task. As the priest-nation, she is to mediate God's blessing to his world. The same idea is found in the oracles of the post-exilic prophet Zechariah:

These are the words of the Lord of Hosts: In those days, ten people from nations of every language will take hold of the robe of one Jew and say, "Let us accompany you, for we have heard that God is with you."

Zechariah 8:23

For post-exilic Israel, then, the world was her parish, for it was God's world, and all nations were part of his creation to be brought within the elect community which ultimately is humankind itself.

Finally, we should note the oracle that occurs in Isaiah 2:2–4 and Micah 4:1–4, where an extra verse is added:

In days to come
the mountain of the Lord's house
will be established higher than all other mountains,
towering above other hills.
Peoples will stream towards it;
many nations will go, saying,
"Let us go up to the mountain of the Lord,
to the house of Jacob's God,
that he may teach us his ways,
and we may walk in his paths."
For instruction issues from Zion,
the word of the Lord from Jerusalem.
He will be judge between the many peoples
and arbiter among great and distant nations.
They will hammer their swords into mattocks
and their spears into pruning-knives.
Nation will not take up sword against nation;
they will never again be trained for war.
Each man will sit under his own vine
or his own fig tree, with none to cause alarm.
The Lord of Hosts himself has spoken.

Micah 4:1–4

It is very unlikely that these universalistic ideas belong to the eighth century. Rather they appear to be a product of the post-exilic vision of Israel's world role inserted into the works of earlier prophets. The oracle does not think of Jerusalem as a centre of political power over other nations, but as a medium of religious instruction which results in a cessation of war and the reuse of redundant weaponry for peaceful purposes. In this way Israel fulfils her vocation securing *shalom* for all peoples.

v. The Priestly Work

We have already seen that decisive political events in effect determined Israel's theology demanding reassessment of her relationship with her God. The establishment of the Davidic monarchy required a document of title to bind the disparate groups that made up the new nation under the invading God, Yahweh, who was understood to have established the kingdom through his grace and would continue to bless his chosen people.

But the loss of the northern kingdom to Assyria, into whose empire she was absorbed, threw such an understanding into question. To southern theologians, God's grace could not be unconditional. Instead they interpreted Yahweh as Israel's suzerain and saw her as his vassal whose future existence depended on obedience to covenant law. Their new theology was redacted into the document of title with the insertion of the making of the covenant, the story of the golden calf, the breaking of the tablets of the law and their replacement, and is reflected in Hezekiah's reform.

The Babylonian conquest led to another reassessment by the Deuteronomists which resulted in an entirely new work, Deuteronomy, Joshua–2 Kings, and the editing of Jeremiah, in which covenant theology was even more strongly reaffirmed and is reflected in Josiah's far more sweeping reform, with its centralisation of all worship at Jerusalem.

But now in exile, theologians whom scholars have termed priestly because of the contents of their work were again forced to reconsider Israel's relationship with Yahweh. Under covenant theology it should have been terminated for all time, as the curses of Deuteronomy made plain (Deuteronomy 28:15–68). Yet as we have seen, both additions to Deuteronomy and Jeremiah questioned such hopelessness and Ezekiel and Deutero-Isaiah looked forward to a positive future. So it was in exile that another radical redaction of the document of title took place, in which it was recognised that Yahweh could not abandon his people. He was a God of grace and could be no other. Through the priestly theologians, the law which had always been seen as an instrument of grace (Deuteronomy 4:8) now ceased to be an instrument of judgment on God's chosen people.

The priestly theologians substantially added to the revised document of title from Hezekiah's time, resulting in what scholars have termed the Tetrateuch, the first four books of the Hebrew Scriptures, Genesis, Exodus, Leviticus and Numbers. The events of Sinai are not seen as the inauguration of a new relationship between Yahweh and the Hebrew slaves, but simply as the fulfilment of the promise to Abraham. These theologians recognised that failure was inherent in man, but the cult with, in particular, its Day of Atonement (Leviticus 16) provided the means whereby Israel might ever renew and reform herself, and so be the people whom God desired her to be. The priestly legislation contained in Leviticus, Numbers and important additions to Exodus was therefore designed to ensure the proper ordering of cult and people. The law therefore protected the existing and permanent relationship of God and Israel from abuse. But it did not create that relationship and nor did it determine its duration. The new covenant of Jeremiah written on the hearts was for ever.

For the priestly theologians, the Abraham narratives, which with the Deuteronomic emphasis on the Sinai covenant had become of less significance, now find a new importance. In the original document of title, it is clear that Abraham is associated with Harran in north-west Mesopotamia. Indeed, Genesis 12:4 asserts that it is from Harran that the patriarch set out for Canaan. The priestly theologians now insert a prior journey, first locating Abraham in Ur of the Chaldees in south-east Mesopotamia (Genesis 15:7). Their purpose is to enable the exiles to identify themselves with the father of the nation. As Yahweh had brought Abraham from distant Ur, identified with Babylon, to Canaan, so he could bring the exiles too, if only they had sufficient faith. Even in the uncertain situation which they faced in a heathen foreign land, the original promise to the patriarch remained valid (Genesis 15). They could yet enjoy land and progeny.

And to confirm this, the priestly theologians created the making of a second and "everlasting" covenant, not only with Abraham but with all generations to come (Genesis 17). They did this by using circumcision, now in non-Semitic Babylon a rite which distinguished the exiles from their captors. As we saw earlier, circumcision was originally a puberty rite associated with marriage and widely performed in the Near East. The priestly theologians transform this practice by ordering that it be performed eight days after birth, so becoming a sign that the male child is part of the elect community from the beginning of his life. It becomes a fundamental testimony of faith.

Finally, in the preface to their work, the priestly theologians make absolutely clear that nothing can invalidate Israel's election, which in fact was part of the very act of creation itself. This explains why the Eden narrative is preceded by another creation account (Genesis 1–2:4a). Taking over an eight-day Babylonian creation story, the priestly theologians compress this to six days—in days three and six two acts of creation take place—so that on the seventh day they could record the inauguration of the Sabbath. This had long been practised in Israel (Amos 8:4–6), but in Babylon was another distinguishing mark of Israelite faith. By making the Sabbath the seventh act of creation, the authors showed that it was as fixed in God's scheme of things as sun and moon, sea and land, animals and humankind. And since the only people in the world who kept the Sabbath were the Jews, they too were fixed in God's creation: their election was established not with Abraham, nor with Moses, nor David, but in the very act of creation itself. They are part of its very fabric and just as it is inconceivable that sun and moon might cease to exist, so it is inconceivable that Israel would cease to be. At the same time, the Deuteronomic linking of the Sabbath commandment to Israel's slavery in Egypt (Deuteronomy 5:12–15) was replaced by reference to God resting on the seventh day of creation (Exodus 20:8–11).

The observation has often been made that the Tetrateuch lacks a climax, namely the Hebrews' entry into the land. Instead, it ends with Moses and the people camped in Moab on the edge of the promised land (Numbers 33:50–51). But this is deliberate, for although the priestly theologians have reaffirmed Israel's unconditional election, that indeed she is integral to creation itself, the people addressed by the Tetrateuch, that is the next generation of exiles, have to appropriate the promise for themselves. God can promise, but whether that promise is realised is in the end for his people to determine. They have to respond to his grace.

Further, the priestly legislation would ensure for a restored Israel the purity of both cult and community. While anyone could become a member of that community irrespective of previous race, colour or religion by agreeing to obey the law, those individuals who failed in any fundamental way must, of necessity, be expelled to ensure its purity. The restored Israel would no longer be a national political entity, but rather a worshipping community centred on the rebuilt temple in Jerusalem.

Probably not long after the return from exile (538), Deuteronomy became detached from its position as an introduction to Joshua–2 Kings and was joined to the Tetrateuch to form the Pentateuch, the first five books of the Hebrew Scriptures, known to Jews as the Torah. Here was the law which prescribed how the restored community was to live. Inevitably in this process, these two quite separate literary works have influenced each other and editing can be discerned. So, for instance, the death of Moses, originally thought to be found at the end of Numbers, now concludes Deuteronomy, Moses having first taken possession of the promised land by looking over it, the normal way land was transferred in Israel (Deuteronomy 34). And it is as a result of Deuteronomy being attached to the Tetrateuch that, in Exodus 34:28, the words on the second set of tablets are described as the Ten Commandments, as they were in Deuteronomy, but not in the exodus narrative of the golden calf, the breaking of the original tablets of the law and their replacement.

So we have now isolated what is in effect the "gospel" of the Hebrew Scriptures. It is the triumphant assertion, worked out through the bitter history of the pre-exilic nation state of Israel and realised in the powerless post-exilic community centred on her temple, that God's grace is what alone sustains humankind, a grace that is there for all to enjoy if only they will appropriate it for themselves. And what is more, in his law, he has provided the means for that enjoyment. This is indeed *good news.*

There is one more aspect of ancient Israel's understanding of her God that needs exploring. Though we have clearly established that God wants humankind to be in relationship with him, it is also clear that we remain part of the created order and so dependent on him. This being so, in what sense can we know God? Are there any necessary limitations to the kind of belief which we can have? To this problem we must now turn.

CHAPTER 6

The Nature of Faith

i. Wisdom

Alongside priest and prophet, there was in ancient Israel a third professional class, the wise (Jeremiah 18:18), who by their advice sought to achieve an ordered existence both for society at large and individuals personally. The wise recognised that God had created the world out of chaos and established a divine order. It was for men and women to conform to that order if they were to enjoy the peace, harmony and wholeness (summed up in the Hebrew word *shalom)* intended for them by God. The counsel of the wise therefore concerned every facet of public and private life. The wise sought to see the order in things: how one thing related to another, how society functioned, how the natural world and science worked. They looked at relationships, objects and ideas and tried to discern their pattern, their structure and their order. Their concern was that men and women should lead the best possible lives, and not come to any mishap. Above all, the wise were expected to be able to so manipulate words that order might be maintained or restored. They knew what to say in a fraught situation, and by saying it brought about *shalom.*

The most famous example of the exercise of wisdom is Solomon's judgement in the case of the two prostitutes and the one surviving child (1 Kings 3). Here was a chaotic situation which seemed impossible to solve, two women both claiming a baby as their own. Yet Solomon, by wise words, was able to bring order out of chaos and restore the child to its rightful mother.

Folly, on the other hand, is failure to see the order in things, resulting in a breakdown of *shalom*. A good example is the story of Nabal (1 Samuel 25), whose name means Fool. He was a rich sheep farmer whose flocks had been protected by David and his men. When David sends his men to get their cut, Nabal churlishly rejects their request, which leads David to resolve to annihilate Nabal and his shepherds. He is only saved by the intervention of his pretty wife, Abigail. Nabal had failed to recognise the order in the arrangement he had made. If someone is employed to protect property and proper payment is refused, the consequences will be dire. As Solomon's words had brought about order, Nabal's had sown disorder.

Wisdom, then, complemented law, for like law it sought to achieve and maintain that divine order which God had inaugurated at creation, but which from the days of Adam was ever threatened by man's folly. Thus, we find in the wisdom literature the same concern for dependent members of society which we saw in the law and the prophets:

> Do not say to your neighbour, "Come back again;
> you can have it to-morrow"—when you could give it now.
>
> *Proverbs 3:28*

> Never rob anyone who is helpless because he is helpless,
> nor ill-treat a poor wretch in court.
>
> *Proverbs 22:22*

> Do not remove an ancient boundary stone
> or encroach on the land of the fatherless.
>
> *Proverbs 23:10*

Further, this literature echoes the prophetic protest in its rejection of the outward forms of religion if these are not accompanied by right actions towards one's neighbour:

> To do what is right and just
> is more acceptable to the Lord than sacrifice.
>
> *Proverbs 21:3*

If anyone turns a deaf ear to God's law,
even his prayer is an abomination.

Proverbs 28:9

However, the main feature of post-exilic wisdom literature, Proverbs, Ecclesiastes, Job and the Psalter, perhaps as a result of Israel's longer-than-expected exile in Babylon, is its preoccupation with the issue of whether men and women get their just deserts. Looking at the world around them, the wise found it increasingly difficult to justify God's ways. How could orthodox theology continue to maintain that there was a moral order in the world for which God was responsible?

ii. Proverbs and Ecclesiastes

Proverbs takes an optimistic view of life unquestioningly accepting the orthodox doctrine of rewards, that it is the guilty who suffer, while the righteous are blessed:

The good man wins the Lord's favour,
the schemer his condemnation.
No mischief will befall the righteous,
but the wicked get their fill of adversity.

Proverbs 12:2, 21

Honour the Lord with your wealth
and with the first fruits of all your produce;
then your granaries will be filled with grain
and your vats will brim with new wine.

Proverbs 3:9–10

Such is the author's faith that he confidently counsels men against taking the law into their own hands. God himself will act as the avenger:

> Do not think to repay evil for evil;
> wait for the Lord to deliver you.
>
> *Proverbs 20:22*

Men and women can place their whole trust in Yahweh:

> Many seek audience of a ruler,
> but it is the Lord who decides each case.
>
> *Proverbs 29:26*

While business acumen will ensure prosperity, happiness lies not in one's natural abilities but in trusting God:

> He who is shrewd in business will prosper,
> but happy is he who puts his trust in the Lord.
>
> *Proverbs 16:20*

Ecclesiastes, on the other hand, boldly recognises that the facts of life do not always measure up to orthodox theological claims. Its conclusion is therefore decidedly pessimistic:

> I have seen everything that has been done here under the sun; it
> is all futility and a chasing of wind.
>
> *Ecclesiastes 1:14*

In considering the respective fortunes of the living and the dead, the author recognises a third group of people even better off—the unborn:

> I accounted the dead happy because they were already dead,
> happier than the living who still have lives to live; more fortunate
> than either I reckoned those yet unborn, who have not witnessed
> the wicked deeds done here under the sun.
>
> *Ecclesiastes 4:2–3*

The author concludes that life is utterly capricious, and the wisest course open to humankind is to try and be on good terms with God, keep his commandments, and hope for the best. There is nothing one can do to insure against the possibility of disaster, for there is in fact no moral order in the world:

> There is a futile thing found on earth: sometimes the just person gets what is due to the unjust, and the unjust what is due to the just. I maintain that this too is futility. So I commend enjoyment, since there is nothing good for anyone to do here under the sun but to eat and drink and enjoy himself; this is all that will remain with him to reward his toil throughout the span of life which God grants him here under the sun.
>
> *Ecclesiastes 8:14–15*

> One more thing I have observed here under the sun: swiftness does not win the race nor strength the battle. Food does not belong to the wise, nor wealth to the intelligent, nor success to the skilful; time and chance govern all. Moreover, no one knows when his hour will come; like fish caught in the destroying net, like a bird taken in a snare, so the people are trapped when misfortune comes suddenly on them.
>
> *Ecclesiastes 9:11–12*

There is though an alternative to the naïve optimism of Proverbs and the negative pessimism of Ecclesiastes to which we must now turn.

iii. Job

The Book of Job consists of a Prologue (1–2) and Epilogue (42:7–16), originally part of a much older tale with something of a fairy tale atmosphere about it, into which has been inserted the Dialogue between Job and his friends (3–27, 29–31), a wisdom poem (28), the interruption of a young man (32–37) and the judgment of God (38–42:6).

The Prologue pictures Job as a man of outstanding piety, entirely righteous and innocent of all sin, an example to all. As a result, as orthodox theology would expect, he enjoys great possessions and numerous offspring, a sure sign of God's special blessing. The Satan, better translated as the Adversary, who is not to be thought of as the devil of later theology, but as a more-than-averagely intelligent member of the divine court, asks God some awkward questions about Job and his relationship with God. He argues that if Job were to suffer loss of all that he has, property and family, he would commit the ultimate sin, curse God to his face. He knows Job to be innocent of any offence, but he believes that his faith cannot be disinterested. God gives consent to a test which Job passes with flying colours, saying:

> Naked I came from the womb,
> naked I shall return whence I came.
> The Lord gives and the Lord takes away;
> blessed be the name of the Lord.
>
> *Job 1:21*

This leads the Adversary to try again when he persuades God to let him physically afflict Job, provided he spares his life. Yet even though he is covered in sores from head to foot, Job refuses to curse God, even when encouraged by his wife to do so: "Why do you still hold fast to your integrity? Curse God, and die!" (Job 2:9).

In effect, viewing the hopelessness of his situation and deducing that there is now no point in him prolonging his life, she was urging Job to commit suicide, for the Hebrews believed that God would automatically strike the blasphemer dead. But Job replies:

> You talk as any impious woman might talk. If we accept good from God, shall we not accept evil?
>
> *Job 2:10*

And the narrator sums up:

> Throughout all this, Job did not utter one sinful word.
>
> *Job 2:10*

Job condemns his wife for her inability to see the order in things. She cannot discern that of necessity life has its ups and downs. Having experienced the goodness of God in the past, it is simply illogical to renounce him now when things have gone so terribly wrong. So despite the apparent injustice of his position, simply by accepting his fate as the will of God, Job passes the Adversary's test in the Prologue itself. His faith is disinterested. Then a very different Job appears in the Dialogue, a Job who is anything but submissive to his lot.

The Prologue concludes with the arrival of the three friends (Job 2:11-13). So hideous was Job's appearance that they did not recognise him. Nor faced with such suffering could they think of anything to say. For seven days and nights the four sat in total silence. In the end Job could stand it no longer. He cannot curse God and die because God has been such a reality to him in the past. Instead he curses the day of his birth, asking God to blot it out of the calendar for all time:

> Perish the day when I was born,
> and the night which said, "A boy is conceived!"
> May that day turn to darkness;
> may God above not look for it,
> nor light of dawn shine on it.
> May gloom and deep darkness claim it again;
> may cloud smother that day, blackness eclipse its sun.
> May blind darkness swallow up that night!
> May it not be counted among the days of the year
> or reckoned in the cycle of the months.
>
> *Job 3:2-6*

To understand the Dialogue it is necessary to recognise that it is couched as a lawsuit in which Job appears as the plaintiff representing himself, and the three friends as advocates for the defendant, God. In effect, what is on trial is God's morality as pronounced by traditional theology: suffering is the result of sin. The problem for Job is that God persistently refuses to appear in court.

There is little connection between the speeches of the two parties, which invariably begin with rhetorical abuse typical of law court technique. Such is Bildad's complaint that, although Job goes on at length, his speech lacks any content:

> How long will you go on saying such things,
> those long-winded ramblings of an old man?
>
> *Job 8:2*

So also is Job's sarcastic mockery of the friends:

> No doubt you are intelligent people,
> and when you die, wisdom will perish!
> But I have sense, as well as you:
> in no way do I fall short of you;
> what gifts indeed have you that others have not?
>
> *Job 12:2–3*

And Eliphaz tells Job that he will not try to emulate his advocacy:

> Would a sensible person give vent to such hot-air arguments
> or puff himself up with an east wind?
> Would he bandy useless words
> and speeches so unprofitable?
>
> *Job 15:2–3*

For Job, the friends' arguments are merely trivial:

> I have heard such things so often before!
> You are trouble-makers one and all!
> You say, "Will this windbag never have done?"
> or "What makes him so stubborn in argument?"
> If you and I were to change places, I could talk as you do;
> how I could harangue you and wag my head at you!
>
> *Job 16:2–4*

The parties do not engage in serious debate to establish a truth at present unknown. Rather each side adopts a rigidly pre-determined position and seeks to silence the other by the force of his case. Since there is no development of the argument, each brief can be examined independently of the other.

What is the substance of the action? Merely from the Prologue it seems to be the possibility of disinterested religion in the face of innocent suffering. Yet that issue has already been settled by Job's reply to his wife. He is not going to be so foolish as only to acknowledge God when things are going well for him. His faith is genuine. But the Dialogue uses the problem of unjust suffering as the framework for a much deeper question, which is the nature of the relationship between men and women and their God. It asks the fundamental question: What kind of belief can we have? Job's faith is no longer at issue. His refusal to commit suicide, but instead put God on trial, confirms that. Rather it is traditional religion, which claims to have all the answers, that finds itself in the dock.

Before examining the cases of the parties, we should note that the possibility of a future life in which the world's wrongs will be righted with rewards and punishments does not enter the debate. The most that the Hebrew hoped for was that, in Eliphaz's words:

> You will know that your descendants will be many
> and your offspring like grass, thick on the earth.
> You will come to the grave in sturdy old age
> as sheaves come in due season to the threshing-floor.

Job 5:25–26

This is the reward that Job receives in the Epilogue (Job 42:16–17). For the Hebrew, life was carried on in his descendants. It was his name—that is, his personality—that lived on, while he descended to the shadowy life of Sheol, the Pit of the Psalms. Despite Handel's use of Job 19:25, "I know that my Redeemer liveth", the book remains strictly orthodox on the doctrine of Sheol and the afterlife:

> As a cloud breaks up and disperses,
> so no one who goes down to Sheol ever comes back;
> he never returns to his house,
> and his abode knows him no more.

Job 7:9–10

> If a tree is cut down,
> there is hope that it will sprout again
> and fresh shoots will not fail.
> Though its root becomes old in the earth,
> its stump dying in the ground,
> yet when it scents water it may break into bud
> and make new growth like a young plant.
> But when a human being dies all his power vanishes;
> he expires, and where is he then?
> As the waters of a lake dwindle,
> or as a river shrinks and runs dry,
> so mortal man lies down, never to rise
> until the very sky splits open.
> If a man dies, can he live again?
> He can never be roused from this sleep.
> If only you would hide me in Sheol,
> conceal me until your anger is past,
> and only then fix a time to recall me to mind!
> I would not lose hope, however long my service,
> waiting for my relief to come.

Job 14:7–14

The whole point of the last two verses is that they envisage something that is utterly impossible. In fact, the Hebrew of Job 19:25–27 is notoriously difficult, as the REB rendering illustrates:

> But I know that my vindicator lives
> and that he will rise last to speak in court;
> I shall discern my witness standing at my side
> and see my defending counsel, even God himself,
> whom I shall see with my own eyes,
> I myself and no other.

But in any event, life after death with the promise of rewards and punishments does not in fact solve the problem of unjust suffering, though it has served to blunt the proper questioning of the morality of the God who has failed to prevent it. Job believes because he knows God now, not because he will know him hereafter. He has no expectation of any future rewards in an afterlife. He has enjoyed the blessings of his relationship with God, which inexplicably and for no good reason God has withdrawn. It is the fundamental nature of this relationship in the here and now which is Job's concern. Can he still believe in a just God in the face of his apparent injustice to him? Is there after all no moral order? What are the facts of life?

Job opens his case by asking why humans were created at all. He cannot "curse God and die" for he has known God and enjoyed his blessing. So he curses the day of his birth for bringing him to this conflict between on the one hand the unfairness of his plight and on the other his previous experience of the gracious God. For him life has become utterly meaningless and pointless. His position on the refuse tip, covered in sores, an outcast of his community, serves to heighten this. Ironically, Job realises that the only hope left to him is Sheol. Why not get the mockery of living a non-life over now and descend there, where at least there are no illusions:

> There the wicked chafe no more,
> there the tired labourer takes his ease;
> the captive too finds peace there,
> no slave-driver's voice reaches him;
> high and low alike are there,
> even the slave, free from his master.
>
> *Job 3:17–19*

For Job, life no longer seems to be controlled by any moral order. He knows himself to be innocent, yet God has dreadfully afflicted him for no reason at all. Life has become a cruel game in which all the rules appear to have been abandoned in God's favour. Worse still, God does not seem to care enough to offer an explanation of what has happened. So Job pleads that God would himself enter the witness stand, where he can properly be cross-examined:

> If only I knew how to reach him,
> how to enter his court,
> I should state my case before him
> and set out my arguments in full;
> then I should learn what answer he would give
> and understand what he had to say to me.
> Would he exert his great power to browbeat me?
> No; God himself would never set his face against me.
> There in his court the upright are vindicated,
> and I should win from my judge an outright acquittal.
>
> *Job 23:3–7*

But earlier in the case Job had despairingly concluded that, even if by some means he was able to summon God to appear in court, he would still get away with it:

> If I summoned him to court and he responded,
> I do not believe that he would listen to my plea;
> for he strikes at me for a trifle
> and rains blows on me without cause;
> he leaves me no respite to recover my breath,
> but sates me with bitter thoughts.
> If the appeal is to force, see how mighty he is;
> if to justice, who can compel him to give me a hearing?
> Though I am in the right,
> he condemns me out of my own mouth;
> though I am blameless, he makes me out to be crooked.
>
> *Job 9:16–20*

Such is God's total loss of any sense of morality, the innocent and wicked are treated alike and God finds it funny:

> Blameless, I say; of myself
> I reck nothing, I hold my life cheap.
> But it is all one; therefore I declare,
> "He destroys blameless and wicked alike."
> When a sudden flood brings death,
> he mocks the plight of the innocent.
> When a country is delivered into the power of the wicked,
> he blindfolds the eyes of its judges.
>
> *Job 9:21–24*

Desperately Job pleads with God for the same kind of justice which he would obtain in an earthly court:

> If only there were one to arbitrate between man and God,
> as between a man and his neighbour!
>
> *Job 16:21*

In sharp contrast to his own situation, Job points to the prosperity of the wicked, which he again attributes to a lack of morality on God's part:

> Why do the wicked live on,
> hale in old age, and great and powerful?
> They see their children settled around them,
> their descendants flourishing,
> their households secure and safe;
> the rod of God's justice does not reach them.
>
> *Job 21:7–9*

Worst of all, despite treating God as utterly irrelevant to their lives, the wicked go to Sheol prosperous and in peace. As their sarcastic use of "the Almighty" indicates, God has no power over them:

> They live out their days in prosperity,
> and they go down to Sheol in peace.
> They say to God, "Leave us alone;
> we do not want to know your ways!

> What is the Almighty that we should worship him,
> or what should we gain by entreating his favour?"
> Is not the prosperity of the wicked in their own hands?
> Are not their purposes very different from God's?
>
> *Job 21:13–16*

Those who defend God reply that if the wicked themselves are not punished, then their sons will be. But that will hardly concern the wicked once they are in Sheol. Rather let them receive their just deserts in this life:

> You say, "The trouble a man earns, God reserves for his sons";
> no, let him be paid for it in full and be punished.
> Let his own eyes witness the condemnation come on him;
> may the wrath of the Almighty be the cup he drinks.
>
> *Job 21:19–20*

For Job, there is no moral order in the world, of which his own suffering is just one more example. However, Job need not have worried about God's possible appearance to answer the charges against him, for God makes no attempt to take the witness stand. Job is utterly isolated. No one believes in his innocence, neither wife nor friends, and God remains inexplicably absent. So Job is brought to the test of faith. Will he remain true to the God whom he has known and whose favour he has enjoyed but also to his own integrity—or will he deny one or the other?

The temptation for Job is clear enough—to come down on one side or the other, to deny God or his own innocence. His own situation and the mass of human misery in the world encourage him to the former, the friends' arguments, the latter. Somehow, he must have sinned. Ironically, Eliphaz had recognised at the beginning of the trial that it was faith in God and the integrity of the individual believer that was at issue:

> Does your piety give you no assurance?
> Does your blameless life afford you no hope?
>
> *Job 4:6*

There is in fact only one way open to Job through which he can both affirm his innocence and yet proclaim his trust in God, and at the same time resolve the issue of the trial, namely through the self-curse. The Hebrews believed that divine action must follow every curse. So Job curses not God but himself. He lists every conceivable wrong which he might have committed and for which God could be punishing him. The long list of offences is set out in Job 31, of which the following are examples:

> If my heart has been enticed by a woman
> or I have lurked by my neighbour's door ...
> If I have withheld from the poor what they needed
> or made the widow's eye grow dim with tears;
> if I have eaten my portion of food by myself,
> and the fatherless child has not shared it with me.
>
> *Job 31:9, 16–17*

If God can show that Job is guilty of any of these charges, then he will accept his present position as just, for he could no longer maintain that he was suffering unfairly. He deserved his punishment and the three friends would be vindicated. But by listing the offences by way of the curse-formula, Job makes it impossible for God to go on avoiding the trial. Through the curse, he has directly challenged God, who has no option but to condemn or acquit Job. Despite God's persistent absence, the lawsuit must now have a verdict. To the end, Job has kept his integrity:

> I swear by the living God, who has denied me justice,
> by the Almighty, who has filled me with bitterness,
> that so long as there is any life left in me
> and the breath of God is in my nostrils,
> no untrue word will pass my lips,
> nor will my tongue utter any falsehood.
> Far be it from me to concede that you are right!
> Till I cease to be, I shall not abandon my claim of innocence.
> I maintain and shall never give up the rightness of my cause;
> So long as I live, I shall not change.
>
> *Job 27:2–6*

Job is forced in the agony of the absence and hostility of God to make the ultimate decision. Either he can commit suicide as his wife advised or he can affirm his faith when there appears no reason to do so. Despised and rejected by all, he triumphantly commits himself in the only way open to him. He affirms his belief both in the God who appears to have rejected him and in his own integrity. Immediately he will know God's presence again.

The three friends act as counsel for the defence of the accused God. As one would expect, they essentially present the same arguments. Their case is simple: suffering is the inevitable result of sin. Job must have offended and is being properly punished. As Eliphaz puts it:

> For consider, has any innocent person ever perished?
> Where have the upright ever been destroyed?
>
> *Job 4:7*

One must trust God:

> For my part, I would make my appeal to God;
> I would lay my plea before him.
>
> *Job 5:8*

Eliphaz even goes so far as to counsel Job to rejoice in his suffering:

> Happy indeed are they whom God rebukes!
> Therefore do not reject the Almighty's discipline.
> For, though he wounds, he will bind up;
> the hands that harm will heal.
>
> *Job 5:17–18*

As a result of their theology, the three friends cannot accept Job's plea of innocence. So Bildad argues:

> Does God pervert justice?
> Does the Almighty pervert what is right?
>
> *Job 8:3*

For as Zophar points out, Job should be punished even more for his presumptuousness in challenging God's justice:

> You claim that your opinions are sound;
> you say to God, "I am spotless in your sight."
> But if only God would speak
> and open his lips to reply,
> to expound to you the secrets of wisdom,
> for wonderful are its achievements!
> Know then that God extracts from you
> less than your sin deserves.
> Can you fathom the mystery of God,
> or attain to the limits of the Almighty?
> They are higher than the heavens. What can you do?
> They are deeper than Sheol. What can you know?
>
> *Job 11:4–8*

In the opinion of the three friends, Job's case should never have been brought. God is unknowable save in what he wills to disclose. Job as a mere mortal cannot begin to understand God and it is sheer arrogance to try. So Eliphaz asks:

> Were you the firstborn of mankind,
> brought forth before the hills?
> Do you listen in God's secret council
> or usurp all wisdom for yourself alone?
> What do you know that we do not know?
> What insight have you that we do not have?
>
> *Job 15:7–9*

As far as Eliphaz is concerned, Job's questioning of God is not only improper but utterly outrageous:

> What makes you so bold at heart,
> and why do your eyes flash,

that you vent your anger on God
and pour out such mouthfuls of words?

Job 15:12–13

The friends are, of course, correct in holding that God cannot be the subject of a legal suit. That does not though mean that it was improper for Job to question him when the facts of life no longer reflected his understanding of the God he had long known. While the friends continue to make the assumption that since God is just, Job's suffering must be the result of sin on his part, Job knows this to be untrue and through the curse-formula submits himself to God's judgment, thereby neither denying his faith nor his integrity. Through continuing to assert his belief in the justice of God when he had no reason to do so, he will once again, even more richly than before, enjoy God's blessing.

The rigours of the Dialogue are followed by the speeches of the young Elihu (Job 32–37). As neither Job nor the friends react to these speeches, it is probably right to see them as inserted here because a later generation felt it improper that the omnipotent and transcendent God should immediately obey Job's summons to explain himself—though the curse-formula necessitated this. In fact, the speeches add little to the Dialogue save to try and justify suffering from the discipline it can engender. However, there is much suffering in the world that cannot be covered in this way—suffering leading to lunacy, for instance. While suffering can be used positively once it has arisen, that does not explain why it should have to occur in the first place.

Then the reader gets what he has been waiting for—the judgment of God. From the book's beginning he has known that God must answer Job's indictment: the trial must have a verdict. By uttering the self-curse, Job has forced God's hand. He now appears in all his might and majesty and answers Job.

The surprise is that far from a simple vindication of Job—whom the reader of the book knows all along to have been innocent—God, in very much the same language as the three friends (Job 11:7–12; 15:7–16), proclaims his utter transcendence and confirms that men and women cannot know as God knows:

Where were you when I laid the earth's foundations?
Tell me, if you know and understand.
Who fixed its dimensions? Surely you know!
Who stretched a measuring line over it?
On what do its supporting pillars rest?
Who set its corner-stone in place,
while the morning stars sang in chorus
and the sons of God all shouted for joy?

Job 38:4-7

As we saw at the beginning of this study, the Eden narrative, as a preface to Israel's document of title, laid down by the use of the two trees the perimeters of what it means to be human. Men and women are mortal and cannot know as God knows. While they can seek to discover everything within creation itself, there are mysteries which God alone can know because he is outside the system he has created.

God's speeches make no attempt either to find guilt on Job's part or admit God's injustice. The tension which Job has discovered is to be maintained, not dissipated. In the face of God's onslaught from the storm, Job acknowledges that he cannot know as God knows. It was presumptuous to have thought otherwise:

Job answered the Lord:
I know that you can do all things
and that no purpose is beyond you.
You ask: Who is this obscuring counsel yet lacking knowledge?
But I have spoken of things
which I have not understood,
things too wonderful for me to know.
Listen, and let me speak. You said:
I shall put questions to you, and you must answer.
I knew of you then only by report,
but now I see you with my own eyes.
Therefore I yield,
repenting in dust and ashes.

Job 42:1-6

Even if the translation of Job 42:6 is correct, and there is some doubt about this, this verse is not to be understood as Job repenting of his presumptuousness in putting God in the dock. Such a conclusion would make nonsense of the book. What has occurred in Job's encounter with the living God is a radical change of attitude on his part, rather than any remorse over guilt. Job acknowledges the limitations of what it means to be human. Job has been right to reject the false answers of the friends, even though their answers were sanctioned by orthodox theology: he had been right to argue with God and force him to appear to answer his indictment. Job's error lay in the assumption that when God did appear he would offer Job an explanation for his suffering. Instead, in coming to Job, God confirms that he remains God and Job remains man:

> Then the Lord answered Job out of the tempest:
> Brace yourself and stand up like a man;
> I shall put questions to you, and you must answer.
> Would you dare deny that I am just,
> or put me in the wrong to prove yourself right?
> Have you an arm like God's arm;
> can you thunder with a voice like his?
>
> *Job 40:6–9*

But by answering Job, God shows that he stands with him in the fullness of his misery, though he does not explain why he should have to endure it. He is in effect told that faith means belief "in spite of", in spite of the apparent injustices which inevitably afflict men and women and for which no explanation can be offered. This is the nature of God's relationship with humankind. In risking all through his self-curse, Job discovers the necessity of an agnostic faith.

So God specifically rewards Job for what he has *said*, that is his prosecution of God with unrestrained ferocity, sarcasm and passion:

> When the Lord had finished speaking to Job, he said to Eliphaz
> the Temanite, "My anger is aroused against you and your two

friends, because, unlike my servant Job, you have not spoken as you ought about me."

Job 42:7

In contrast, the three friends are condemned and have to rely on Job's prayers for their acceptance by God again. While they rested their case on the proper doctrine of the transcendence of God, they failed to enter into the reality of Job's experience, but denied it. So, ironically, those who had relied on traditional theology to defend God in the end find that they are forced to depend on the man who, in the face of overwhelming suffering, would neither deny God nor his own innocence:

> Now take seven bulls and seven rams, go to my servant Job and offer a whole-offering for yourselves, and he will intercede for you. I shall surely show him favour by not being harsh with you because you have not spoken as you ought about me, as he has done.

Job 42:8

So while the Prologue concerned the man who meekly accepted his suffering, showing that disinterested religion was possible, the Dialogue pictures a very different situation. But the trial gives no answer to the problem of unjust suffering nor why some people should suffer and not others. Over some things we have to remain agnostic, though we can be agnostic believers. That is the nature of faith.

Indeed, the Book of Job tells us much more about being human than about God. For men and women, in their ability to express faith, are every bit as much a mystery as God. As Job ironically points out:

> What is man, that you make much of him
> and turn your thoughts towards him,
> only to punish him morning after morning
> or to test him every hour of the day?

Job 7:17–18

So Job is not afraid to point out that men and women are as necessary to God as God is to them. As he reminds God, should anything untoward happen to him, it would be God who would be every bit as much the loser:

> Why do you not pardon my offence
> and take away my guilt?
> For soon I shall lie in the dust of the grave;
> you may seek me, but I shall be no more.
>
> *Job 7:21*

Thus, oddly enough, in contrast to the facile optimism of the Book of Proverbs, the conclusion of Job is very similar to that of Ecclesiastes. Life is unfair, good men and women do suffer unjustly, there is apparently no moral order—but in spite of this one can still know God. For Ecclesiastes, this is a pessimistic conclusion, for Job optimistic, for Job recognises that knowledge of God is the one thing that matters for the wise person. This is neatly summed up in the wisdom poem in Job 28, itself a late addition to the book. Here, against the simile of mining for precious metals, and in contradiction to Proverbs 2:1–5, wisdom is presented as being quite beyond human discovery: only God knows the way to it. Wisdom belongs to him alone: he alone has all the answers. Yet God does choose to enter into relationship with men and women. This is the meaning of the closing couplet of the poem:

> The fear of the Lord is wisdom,
> and to turn from evil, that is understanding!
>
> *Job 28:28*

It is through religion, "the fear of the Lord", that men and women find that order, peace and harmony which they seek, and which they cannot experience otherwise within this disordered world. How that disorder arose, the Book of Job does nothing to explain.

Of all the wisdom literature Job is the most profound, for the author brings home to men and women what must of necessity be the nature of their faith. For although Job ends up in the same position as his three friends, unable to place God in the dock, he knows as the friends do not know, that the believer is an agnostic too. He is freed from the necessity of having to give an explanation for everything. Job affirms that knowledge of God and knowledge of all the answers about God are two different things. Men and women can in fact only have the former—they can only be agnostic believers. Job's witness to both his faith and his integrity, despite all the evidence to the contrary, could only result in God's blessing:

> The Lord restored Job's fortunes, and gave him twice the possessions he had before ... Thus the Lord blessed the end of Job's life more than the beginning.
>
> *Job 42:10, 12*

iv. The Psalter

The Psalter is a collection of 150 psalms divided into five books, probably to be set alongside the five books of Moses, the Pentateuch. While some psalms are pre-Israelite, being inherited from Canaan (Psalms 29, 68), others are very late, such as the two law psalms 1 and 119. It is usually thought that the Psalter was formed in the second century. This was a very uncertain time for Israel and explains why, despite its Hebrew title *tehillim*, meaning songs of praise, laments dominate the collection.

That the Psalter is a selection of available material is clear from the presence of further psalms in the Hebrew Scriptures themselves. Examples are the prayer of Hannah said in thanksgiving for Samuel's birth (1 Samuel 2:1–10) and the prayer of Jonah when swallowed by the large fish (Jonah 2:2–9). In both cases narrators have put into the mouths of their characters psalms deemed appropriate to their situation.

It has long been recognised that the psalms fall into different categories—hymns of praise; communal laments; psalms concerning the king; individual laments; individual thanksgivings. Rather than seeing them as reflecting particular historical events as their titles might imply, they are to be understood in terms of Israel's worshipping life, as references to the temple, processions, sacrifice, dancing, singing and music confirm. Indeed, the titles are in the main best seen as an early form of biblical exegesis, as attempts were made to identify the occasion when they were first uttered. While some may go back to the time of David, few scholars would want to ascribe the authorship of any particular psalm to him. The association of David with the psalms, like the association of Solomon with wisdom sayings, reflects the traditions found in the Books of Samuel and Kings, in which David plays the harp and Solomon asks God for the gift of wisdom.

My concern is to examine those psalms that reflect the issues raised in the wisdom literature of which many psalms form a part, and in particular mirror the Book of Job. Like that literature, these psalms recognise that life is brutish and unfair, often in contrast to the success of the wicked or enemies. Further, the wretched circumstances in which the Psalmist finds himself are by no means always the result of sin, but can be laid at the door of God himself, a God who so often chooses to absent himself when he is most needed:

> Why stand far off, Lord?
> Why hide away in times of trouble?
>
> *Psalm 10:1*

> How long, Lord, will you leave me forgotten,
> how long hide your face from me?
>
> *Psalm 13:1*

Here in the wretched "Why?" and "How long?" lies the rub of the Psalter which bears witness not only to the God who is present, but also to the God who hides himself from those who wish to know him. While God can be seen in the wonders of his creation and acknowledged in his people's history, all too often he appears not only no longer master of his kingdom, but indifferent to its full realisation. Time and again the Psalmist encounters a radical disparity between his religious convictions and the realities of his own experiences. These are the unpleasant facts of life with which the Psalter confronts both God and the would-be believer.

The challenge comes on two issues which are two sides of the same coin: (i) why do the faithful suffer? and (ii) why do the wicked prosper?

These questions are not asked in an academic, abstract manner in the quiet of the study, but in passion in the sanctuary, hurled at the very God whom the faithful acknowledge but hold responsible for the unfair position which confronts them. Their problem is that having known God's presence in the past, and enjoyed the riches of his blessing, they cannot make sense of his absence now, nor their suffering, often in the face of the success of the wicked.

The communal lament of Psalm 44 provides a good example. It begins by referring to those mighty acts of God which tradition held had established Israel in the land of Canaan:

> We have heard for ourselves, God,
> our forefathers have told us
> what deeds you did in their time,
> all your hand accomplished in days of old.
> To plant them in the land, you drove out the nations;
> to settle them, you laid waste the inhabitants.
> It was not our fathers' swords that won them the land,
> nor did their strong arm give them victory,
> but your right hand and your arm
> and the light of your presence; such was your favour to them.
>
> *vv. 1-3*

But how different things are now:

> Yet you have rejected and humbled us
> and no longer lead our armies to battle.
> You have forced us to retreat before the foe,
> and our enemies have plundered us at will.
> You have given us up to be slaughtered like sheep
> and scattered us among the nations.
> You sold your people for next to nothing
> and had no profit from the sale.
>
> *vv. 9-12*

As in Job, such sarcasm is a mark of many laments. God has not even secured a good bargain for his unjust act. He did not even make an efficient crook. As a result of Israel's fate, it is the heathen nations who are the winners:

> You have exposed us to the contempt of our neighbours,
> to the gibes and mockery of those about us.
> You have made us a byword among the nations,
> and the peoples toss their heads at us.
>
> *vv. 13–14*

Blame for the disaster which the people are now experiencing is not to be laid upon other gods: it is Israel's God who has sole control of events and who has suddenly afflicted her without any justification at all:

> Though all this has befallen us, we do not forget you
> and have not been false to your covenant;
> our hearts have not been unfaithful,
> nor have our feet strayed from your path.
> Yet you have crushed us as the sea serpent was crushed,
> and covered us with deepest darkness.
>
> *vv. 17–19*

This totally inexplicable and unfair situation leads the worshippers to summon their slumbering God to action:

> Rouse yourself, Lord; why do you sleep?
> Awake! Do not reject us for ever.
> Why do you hide your face,
> heedless of our misery and our sufferings?
>
> *vv. 23–24*

There is more sarcasm here: was it not the confident assertion of orthodox theology as set out in Psalm 121:3–4 that:

> He will not let your foot stumble;
> he who guards you will not sleep.
> The guardian of Israel
> never slumbers, never sleeps.

What the Psalter shows is that if faith is to be maintained the worshipper faced with the unpleasant facts of life has no alternative but to question God. He could of course abandon or reject him. Indeed, to accept the situation as it is appears to deny God's morality. Is not rejection of belief better than belief in an utterly capricious God? Faced with the bitter facts of life, the man or woman who wishes to maintain belief has in fact only one choice, belief "in spite of". But that does not dull the protest nor make it any less real.

Of course, suffering is not always inexplicable or to be laid at God's door. Much of it results from man's own fault. Yet it is surprising how rarely the Psalmist attributes suffering to sin. Psalm 69:5 is one example:

> God, you know how foolish I am,
> and my guilty deeds are not hidden from you.

The reason that the Psalms so rarely mention sin as a cause for suffering is that it presents no problem for traditional theology. Even if the sinner was getting more than his just deserts as Psalm 69 implies, nonetheless there was a cause for his suffering. The fact that so many psalms can find no reason for the suffering being experienced, and in contrast point to the prosperity of the wicked, clearly indicates that the Psalmists refused to correlate suffering with sin, nor pass up the severe challenge to faith that resulted from this refusal. For the only faith worth having is a faith which takes into account both the reality of the God whose love one can experience, and the reality of life in a world in which the absence of that love can also be experienced. It is the Psalmist's acceptance of the challenge to a moral God who appears to act immorally in his world that constitutes the greatness of the Psalter.

Both Psalms 10 and 13 take up the double challenge to God: the suffering of the faithful and the success of the wicked. Both begin with agonising cries to the absent God: "Why stand far off, Lord?" (Psalm 10:1)

and "How long, Lord, will you leave me forgotten?" (Psalm 13:1). Because
of God's apparent inactivity, the wicked can ignore God:

> The wicked in their pride do not seek God;
> there is no place for God in any of their schemes.
>
> *Psalm 10:4*

The wicked do not deny God's existence. There were no atheists in the
ancient Near Eastern world. Rather they believe that, as God will not
intervene in their affairs, they can act with impunity, thinking that they
can get away with their wickedness.

Both Psalms 10 and 13 conclude with a statement of faith. But in
neither case are we to assume that God has already acted to relieve the
suffering Psalmist. What these assertions testify is the necessity for
belief "in spite of". Although God has absented himself, the Psalmist
will neither renounce him nor accept the justice of his absence. Rather
he affirms amid all his doubt his belief that in the end God will vindicate
the faithful.

No psalm is more unremittingly bitter than Psalm 88, described as
of unrelieved gloom and anguish. Unlike Psalms 10 and 13, there is
no concluding statement of faith: rather the psalm ends on the most
poignant of notes:

> You have taken friend and neighbour far from me;
> darkness is now my only companion.
>
> *Psalm 88:18*

Yet the remarkable fact that such a psalm finds its place in the Psalter
is a testimony to faith itself. For in reciting it, the worshipper places his
hopeless situation before God. He may not believe that God can or will do
anything about it: he simply holds that he should be faced with the facts.
Despite God's inexplicable action, the suffering believer is still prepared
to confront him:

> You have plunged me into the lowest abyss,
> into the darkest regions of the depths.

> Your wrath bears heavily upon me,
> you have brought on me all your fury.
>
> *Psalm 88:6–7*

He could, of course, have interpreted his fate as a result of sin, but there is no suggestion that he does, or that he suffers from any just cause. Indeed, no attempt is made to explain the irrationality of what has happened. The Psalmist's sole concern is that if he must perish, God too will be the loser:

> Will it be for the dead you work wonders?
> Or can the shades rise up and praise you?
> Will they speak in the grave of your love,
> of your faithfulness in the tomb?
> Will your wonders be known in the region of darkness,
> your victories in the land of oblivion?
>
> *Psalm 88:10–12*

Once more we encounter bitter sarcasm.

It is time now to turn the coin over and consider the success of the wicked. We would be foolish to ignore this as if spiritual men and women should impassively shrug it off. We rightly feel a natural desire for justice. Why is it that those who do not seem to deserve to prosper do so, often at the expense of the righteous? A number of psalms try to pretend that the problem does not exist. So Psalm 1 concludes:

> The Lord watches over the way of the righteous,
> but the way of the wicked is doomed.
>
> *Psalm 1:6*

Anyway, the success of the wicked is only transient:

> I have seen a wicked man inspiring terror,
> flourishing as a spreading tree in its native soil.
> But one day I passed by and he was gone;
> for all that I searched for him, he was not to be found.
>
> *Psalm 37:35–36*

Earlier, Psalm 37 had argued that in the end all would work out alright:

> I have been young and now have grown old,
> but never have I seen the righteous forsaken
> or their children begging bread.
>
> *Psalm 37:25–26*

One is tempted to ask how hard he looked!

Psalm 49 attempts to solve the problem by referring to death, the great leveller. While the wicked may get away with it in their lifetime, in the end they too must die and then they will look pretty foolish:

> For we see that the wise die,
> as the stupid and senseless also perish,
> leaving their wealth to others.
> Though they give their names to estates,
> the grave is their eternal home,
> their dwelling for all time to come.
>
> *Psalm 49:10–11*

But the Psalmist recognises that, at a time when there was no belief in life after death, the weakness of his solution is that this is also the fate of the righteous. At least the wicked get to Sheol, the Pit, that state of limbo where there is no feeling nor sensation, having had a good time: not so the righteous. It is belief in life after death with rewards and punishments which has blunted the Psalmist's challenge to the morality of God. But life after death does not in fact solve the problem of unjust suffering nor the success of the wicked. Future reward cannot justify why some should face unjust and unmerited suffering now. A moral God ought to be able to ensure that such a situation should not occur. We cannot simply shrug off the problem with the promise of rewards hereafter. It is the facts of life which have to be faced, facts which apparently contradict the very nature of the God whom the faithful will to acknowledge.

For our age, as for the age of those who made the Psalter, unjust suffering and the success of the wicked pose the most serious threat to faith. It is though with Psalm 73 that we reach the high point of Hebrew theology within the Psalter. The Psalmist begins by indicating that it was the problem of the success of the wicked which nearly caused him to renounce his faith:

> My feet had almost slipped,
> my foothold had all but given way,
> because boasters roused my envy when I
> saw how the wicked prosper.
>
> *vv. 2–3*

Angrily, he acknowledges that the wicked are at peace with themselves:

> No painful suffering for them!
> They are sleek and sound in body;
> they are not in trouble like ordinary mortals,
> nor are they afflicted like other folk.
>
> *vv. 4–5*

> Such are the wicked;
> unshakeably secure, they pile up wealth.
>
> *v. 12*

But to surrender his faith would have been to deny the tradition in which he had been brought up:

> Had I thought to speak as they do,
> I should have been false to your people.
>
> *v. 15*

Then a change takes place. The Psalmist entered God's sanctuary and experienced his presence. Two things resulted. First, he realised that the prosperity of the wicked was illusory and therefore irrelevant, for they are:

> like a dream when one awakes, Lord,
> like images dismissed when one rouses from sleep!
>
> *v. 20*

Second, the only thing that mattered was the Psalmist's own relationship with his God:

> My mind was embittered,
> and I was pierced to the heart.
> I was too brutish to understand,
> in your sight, God, no better than a beast.
> Yet I am always with you;
> you hold my right hand.
> You guide me by your counsel
> and afterwards you will receive me with glory.
> Whom have I in heaven but you?
> And having you, I desire nothing else on earth.
> Though heart and body fail,
> yet God is the rock of my heart, my portion for ever.
>
> *vv. 21–26*

Faith did not depend on the Psalmist's understanding of God and his ways, but rather on God's grasp of him. And despite all the unpleasant facts of life, there is nothing that can break this relationship against which everything else is utterly insignificant and of transient importance.

The Psalmist had been right to beard God in his sanctuary. Like Job, his error lay in thinking that once he did so, everything would be made plain. In fact, he has misunderstood the nature of God's relationship with humankind. He is denied the fruit of the tree of the knowledge of good and evil.

Nonetheless, God does come to men and women in all the unfairness of life. He wills to embrace them; even if he cannot explain why life is as it is. The two questions remain unanswered, but what the Psalmist discovers is that he can still believe, even if that belief must of necessity be an agnostic faith. But such an insight would never have been gained had not the Psalmist wrestled with the God whom he held responsible for the unfairness of life. So he discovers that, in spite of all the unjustness of life which he still cannot explain, he can know God. And this knowledge is sufficient, for it is in that that true peace is to be found.

The Psalmist thus becomes free from the burden of having to give an explanation for everything. Through his questioning of God, he discovers the paradoxical character of faith—the only kind of faith which in the conditions of this world we can have. There are then no easy answers to questions about the unjust suffering of the righteous or the prosperity of the wicked. Life is not fair and never will be fair. This is a fact of life which believer and non-believer have to live with. There is no way of avoiding the ambiguities of life.

Rather, when we find that our experience of life no longer fits our understanding of the moral God whom we will to affirm, we are to let our doubts, anger and rebellion surface in all their bitterness in the very worship of the apparently indifferent God. Like the Psalmist, there is no need to be polite. For it is in our faithful but frustrated witness among the inconsistencies, confusion and resentments which make up our lives that God's power is manifested, in passion that his rule is realised.

CHAPTER 7

The Nature of Grace

i. Summary

We have now completed our study of the Hebrew Scriptures and traced the development of Israel's understanding of the nature of her God, Yahweh. We saw from the document of title composed in the early years of the Davidic monarchy that initially Israel saw herself as the elect people of God. While her law required not only obedience to provisions which could be enforced through the courts, but also the unenforceable laws of humaneness and righteousness, the Hebrews did not see themselves as under any threat, but the recipients of God's grace with which he willed to embrace them.

The loss of the northern kingdom to Assyria following the eighth-century prophetic protest led to a radical reassessment of Israel's theology. Mistakenly, this disaster led to the belief that the exercise of God's grace could be limited. Drawing on the provisions of the political suzerainty treaty imposed on southern Judah, Israel's relationship with her God was reinterpreted as a strict covenant, obedience to which would determine her future. Grace was limited by threat. So the covenant concept was introduced into Israel's original document of title.

The Babylonian conquest and destruction of Jerusalem, followed by the exile, only reinforced this understanding of the limitation of God's grace, resulting in a new work, Deuteronomy, and its accompanying "history" of the monarchy, Joshua–2 Kings. While logically this theology meant there could be no future for Israel, the very writing of these works showed that hope had not been entirely extinguished. This was reaffirmed by later additions to Deuteronomy itself, as well as the release of Jehoiachin from prison.

In Babylon, exilic theologians rejected the idea that God's grace could be understood in terms of a crude "political" bargain. They recognised that his nature was such that he could not in fact let his people go. Indeed, in the very act of creation, as the institution of the Sabbath showed, Israel's election as the chosen people of God had been ensured for all time, provided she had the faith to believe this. So once more the document of title was edited, thereby confirming its original theological authenticity as witnessing to God's unbreakable commitment to his people.

Further, it was God's will that all humankind should enjoy this election. Therefore, Israel was tasked as priest nation to the world to achieve this. For all humankind had been made in God's image—that is, for relationship with him.

Yet the limitations imposed on men and women at creation remained. As the two trees in Eden indicated, not only are they mortal, they have also to accept an agnostic element in their belief. They cannot know all the answers, particularly the reason for unjust suffering, though they can know God. This is what ultimately matters.

Finally, we must consider in what way Jesus, who claimed as his Father the God of the Hebrew Scriptures, confirms our interpretation of his nature. In doing so, we shall encounter unjust grace.

ii. Jesus and The Law

In his summary of the law, Jesus unequivocally reiterates the dual concerns of Hebrew law:

> "Love the Lord your God with all your heart, with all your soul, and with all your mind." That is the greatest, the first commandment. The second is like it: "Love your neighbour as

yourself." Everything in the law and the prophets hangs on these two commandments.

Matthew 22:37–40

At no point in his ministry did Jesus seek to set aside the law. He recognised it as the God-given means whereby order and harmony were to be maintained within society. No detail was so unimportant as not to warrant complete obedience:

> Do not suppose that I have come to abolish the law and the prophets; I did not come to abolish, but to complete. Truly I tell you: so long as heaven and earth endure, not a letter, not a dot, will disappear from the law until all that must happen has happened.
>
> *Matthew 5:17–18*

But Jesus recognised the limitations of any legal system. It could of necessity cover only specific identifiable actions which could be the subject of legal enforcement through the courts. But much of the chaos in society results from people's inner conflicts, their lusts, hates and jealousies, which lead them to attitudes and actions incompatible with respect for one's neighbour. For Jesus, any thought or action which led to conflict was "illegal", for it broke the fundamental commandment of love. So in the Sermon on the Mount he reinterprets the ancient laws on murder and adultery (Matthew 5:21–30). To hate a man, to lust after a woman, are equally disorderly. Even to act in self-defence or exercise one's legitimate rights would in itself only further chaos and so is ruled out by Jesus (Matthew 5:38–42). Under his law his followers have no rights, for they have surrendered them to the law of love enshrined in the person of Jesus:

> When he was abused he did not retaliate, when he suffered he uttered no threats, but delivered himself up to him who judges justly.
>
> *1 Peter 2:23*

So even one's enemies and persecutors are entitled to claim one's love:

You have heard that they were told, "Love your neighbour and hate your enemy". But what I tell you is this: Love your enemies and pray for your persecutors; only so can you be children of your heavenly Father, who causes the sun to rise on good and bad alike, and sends the rain on the innocent and the wicked. If you love only those who love you, what reward can you expect? Even the tax-collectors do as much as that. If you greet only your brothers, what is there extraordinary about that? Even the heathen do as much. There must be no limit to your goodness, as your heavenly Father's goodness knows no bounds.

Matthew 5:43–48

We have already seen how Hebrew law reflected Israel's understanding of the nature of her God: the same is true of Jesus' interpretation of the law. For as his justification for the requirement of unconditional love indicates, in sustaining humankind God makes no distinction between good and bad. All have an equal claim on his generosity simply because they are those created in his image. Of necessity, his grace is always unjust, given to those who deserve and those who do not, equally. For it is not God's way to further disorder by disorder. Indeed, he is constantly engaged in the cosmic battle against chaos, though in meeting that chaos head on in the incarnation, death, and resurrection of Jesus, he has shown that ultimately order will prevail.

But nothing brought more disorder to Israelite society than the love of wealth. Originally conceived as an egalitarian community, by the time of the eighth-century prophets Israel had become the victim of a rapacious class system in which the poor and dependent were ruthlessly exploited. Jesus also recognised that earthly wealth was the greatest single barrier to fulfilling the heavenly law of love:

How hard it is for the wealthy to enter the kingdom of God! It is easier for a camel to go through the eye of a needle than for a rich man to enter the kingdom of God.

Luke 18:24–25

Not that Jesus, any more than ancient Israel, was puritan. But no one could rest content while they knew that others were in want. The rich man at his table had every right to luxuriate in the good things which God had given him: he had no right to do so while Lazarus lay at his gate starving (Luke 16:19–31). How truly the author of 1 Timothy wrote when he held that "the love of money is the root of all evil" (1 Timothy 6:10). Rather than place their trust in God, men and women seek their own security within the created order, and in doing so further disorder. Yet humankind is not ultimately destined for this world. Their enjoyment of possessions here is of necessity transitory. Faced with a choice between the apparent security of his wealth and the equally apparent insecurity of joining the itinerant rabbi from Nazareth, the rich young man imagines that he plays safe (Matthew 19:16–22). But the futility of his action is nicely illustrated by the parable of the farmer who thought he had ensured his prosperity through a bumper harvest, only to die immediately (Luke 12:16–21). The widow with her mite showed greater perception (Luke 21:1–4). There is in fact nothing more testing of the reality of one's faith than one's attitude towards property and wealth:

> Have no fear, little flock; for your Father has chosen to give you the kingdom. Sell your possessions and give to charity. Provide for yourselves purses that do not wear out, and never-failing treasure in heaven, where no thief can get near it, no moth destroy it. For where your treasure is, there will your heart be also.
>
> *Luke 12:32–34*

The rich young man was clearly a good and attractive person who kept the law and wanted to do the right thing. This was not so with the religious authorities who, while going through the motions of their faith, exploited their fellow men:

> Beware of the scribes, who love to walk up and down in long robes and be greeted respectfully in the street, to have the chief seats in synagogues and places of honour at feasts. Those who eat

up the property of widows, while for appearance sake they say long prayers, will receive a sentence all the more severe.

Mark 12:38–40

Echoing the eighth-century prophetic protest, Jesus vigorously condemns the scribes and Pharisees for their hypocrisy (Matthew 23:23–39). While they readily fulfil the requirements of the law, they neglect the purpose of the law itself, the maintenance of order and harmony within the community. Just as their fathers rejected the prophets, so in their turn will they do the same, and once again bring catastrophe on Jerusalem (Matthew 24:1–2). Further, the religious authorities are even capable of turning law into anti-law. Thus, through spuriously dedicating their property to God, they circumvented the ancient commandment to honour one's parents (Matthew 15:1–9). The frequent conflicts about Sabbath observance are similarly to be explained. The Sabbath had been given by God as a sign of freedom. Israel was no longer subject to the orders of any political power, but only to that divine ordering that God willed for his world. Yet the scribes and Pharisees attempted to use the Sabbath rest to perpetuate disorderly situations. In response to their action, Jesus quoted Hosea 6:6: "It is mercy I require, not sacrifice" (Matthew 12:7). It is not religious practice alone which determines acceptance before God, but also one's conduct to other people. In fact, in their attitude to Sabbath observance, the Pharisees showed that they put property before people, and so rejected the basic principle of Hebrew law which they thought they were so faithfully obeying (Luke 13:10–17).

And Jesus makes it perfectly plain that religion by itself is insufficient:

Not everyone who says to me, "Lord, Lord" will enter the kingdom of Heaven, but only those who do the will of my heavenly Father. When the day comes, many will say to me, "Lord, Lord, did we not prophesy in your name, drive out demons in your name, and in your name perform many miracles?" Then I will tell them plainly, "I never knew you. Out of my sight; your deeds are evil!"

Matthew 7:21–23

No amount of religious activity will make men and women acceptable before God if they fail to fulfil the claims made upon them by their fellow citizens. Before they can rightly worship God, such claims must be met (Matthew 5:23-24). So in the parable of the sheep and goats, Jesus pictures the last judgement being made entirely on very ordinary humanitarian grounds—feeding the hungry, giving drink to the thirsty, clothing the naked, and visiting the sick and those in prison (Matthew 25:31-46).

And for Jesus there was to be no limit set on those who could appeal as of right to the exercise of the commandment to love one's neighbour. For by the parable of the Good Samaritan, which Luke sets immediately after Jesus' summary of the law (Luke 10:25-37), it is made plain that the "neighbour" is no longer to be restricted to one's fellow Jews, as under ancient Israel's law, but is to include any human being in need, simply because he is human.

Jesus thus confirms the attitude of the Old Testament law. Obedience to God includes love of one's neighbour, now redefined as any in need. Human welfare is of eternal significance, whereas personal property is of only transient importance. Indeed, it is the mark of Christians that even over everyday necessities they should exhibit no anxiety (Matthew 6:25-34).

iii. Jesus and "The New Covenant"

Although the post-exilic community of Israel recognised that God was not bound by a threat theology, that he was indeed the God of grace, that did not prevent the exclusion from the community of all those who threatened its purity. While the Day of Atonement (Leviticus 16) provided the means for those within the community to seek God's forgiveness, those forced outside it had no such opportunity. But God cannot be so limited: he who has created all desires all to know his grace, saint and sinner alike. To make this plain, Jesus broke all customary Jewish practice and deliberately sought the company of those whom Judaism had rejected, the tax-collectors who had thrown in their lot with the Roman authorities, and the sinners whose heinous acts had excluded them from Judaism for all time. Again, to justify such action, Matthew makes Jesus quote Hosea 6:6: "I require mercy, not sacrifice" (Matthew 9:13). Judaism of Jesus' day, now under Roman occupation, instead of fulfilling its mission to the world to bring all men and women to the knowledge of the one true God, had turned in on itself, concentrating on ensuring its purity by removing or ceasing to court all who might contaminate its religious life. But that religious life itself was to be condemned by Jesus as empty for its contemptuous attitude to the spiritual needs of men and women. Love for one's neighbour was to transcend all barriers, for, however sinful, all were made in the image of God and so for relationship with him:

> Alas for you, scribes and Pharisees, hypocrites! You shut the door
> of the kingdom of Heaven in people's faces; you do not enter
> yourselves, and when others try to enter, you stop them.
>
> *Matthew 23:13*

It is not the function of the religious to act as a protection society for God. He is quite capable of looking after himself. Rather it is their function so to eradicate disorder that the kingdom can come in all its fullness. But the only way this can be achieved is by love—love which, while still holding fast to the importance of law, yet overrides that law in face of need. Such, say both Old and New Testaments, is God's love.

By his attitude to men like Zacchaeus (Luke 19:1–10) and the woman who anointed him at Simon's house (Luke 7:36–50), Jesus showed that God's love for humankind extended far beyond "the fence of the law". There was in fact no point at which God could let humankind go, for God is love and can be no other. Once more Israel had made her God too small.

The particular sin of the Jewish authorities was to forget that in the end Israel too depended on God's grace. She had not earned her special position, but received it through God's election. But because obedience to the law was the sole criterion for membership of Israel, those who achieved this could all too easily think of their position before God as one of right. They had attained this entirely by their own merit. This attitude is behind the parable of the Pharisee and the tax-collector (Luke 18:9–14). While the Pharisee can stand unflinchingly before God, showing no sense of indebtedness to him, the tax-collector can only throw himself on God's mercy. But it is this man who goes home justified, for he has realised that his acceptance by God is entirely due to God's grace and to no action on his part.

The Pharisee might well have complained that God was unjust. He had devoted his life to obedience of the law:

> I thank you, God, that I am not like the rest of mankind—greedy, dishonest, adulterous—or, for that matter, like this tax-collector. I fast twice a week; I pay tithe on all that I get.
>
> *Luke 18:11–12*

This was the complaint of the elder son in the parable of the prodigal son (Luke 15:11–32). As soon as his wastrel brother appeared in sight, his father rushed out and, before he had uttered a word of remorse, embraced and kissed him. Then allowing the boy the dignity of confession, he has his servants clothe his son in the best robe, place a ring on his finger and sandals on his feet. The fatted calf is killed and the feast begins. Not unreasonably, the elder son, returning from his normal daily work on the farm and finding the festivities already in progress, was furious and refused to take part:

> You know how I have slaved for you all these years; I never once disobeyed your orders; yet you never gave me so much as a kid, to celebrate with my friends. But now that this son of yours turns up, after running through your money with his women, you kill the fatted calf for him.
>
> *Luke 15:29–30*

To this comes the reply:

> "My boy," said the father, "you are always with me, and everything I have is yours. How could we fail to celebrate this happy day?

> Your brother here was dead and has come back to life; he was
> lost and has been found."
>
> *Luke 15:31–32*

What these parables teach us is that God's grace is unjust by human standards. But God is different from humankind. His grace cannot be held back for God is love and love knows no restraint. What the Pharisee in the temple and the elder son needed to recognise was that there will always be "greater joy in heaven over one sinner who repents than over ninety-nine righteous people who do not need to repent" (Luke 15:7). The reason is simple. That sinner allows God to be himself—the God of unfettered grace.

But far from abrogating the law, Jesus, by his reinterpretation of the law in the Sermon on the Mount, showed that in fact men and women were incapable of expressing true order and harmony, which the law was designed to achieve. Being unable to justify themselves before God, they had no alternative but to fall back on his grace, grace which would not be denied to anyone who asked for it. So in the end the Pharisee and the tax-collector, as well as the two brothers, stand in the same position. They represent humankind against God, and all are dependent on him for their acceptance. But the Jewish authorities, rightly sensing that such revolutionary theology threatened their existence, took fright at the full vision of God's love, and got the Romans to crucify it.

Yet even such action could not terminate the covenant of promise. For paradoxically there had been one true Israelite who had fulfilled, as no one else could fulfil, the dual command to love God and his neighbour. It was he who kept the promise of Israel's election alive and who in his person provides the seamless continuity between Old and New Testaments. So once more God's love triumphs over the dead bones of Israel, and the Israel of the "new covenant" is born, the Israel of the resurrection body, the Church. Jesus thus fulfils Israel's calling as the suffering servant who makes atonement between God and humankind (Isaiah 53). For through him, our great high priest, all are seen to be acceptable to God. It is no wonder that the Church took so little time in admitting Gentiles to her ranks, something which Mark anticipated in the Syro-Phoenician woman's rebuke to Jesus: "Even the dogs under the table eat the children's scraps" (Mark 7:28). For the fence of the law would give way to common dependence on the God of grace.

But it remains the besetting sin of the righteous to limit God's love. So even today resort is still made to a mistaken threat theology which holds that refusal in this life to acknowledge God will inevitably result in eternal rejection. God is again made the subject of a crude bargain: men and women are encouraged to follow him out of fear, not love, and the gospel becomes bad news. But the theology of both Old and New Testaments points to a God who cannot let go, a God who will stop at nothing to bring all into relationship with himself. For just when some thought they could draw a line whereby they could limit love, they found that God went through it and beyond it. So Ezekiel saw God re-create Israel from dry bones; the apostles witnessed the breakdown of the fence of the law. As Faber's hymn puts it:

> For the love of God is broader,
> Than the measures of man's mind;
> And the heart of the Eternal
> Is most wonderfully kind.
> But we make his love too narrow
> By false limits of our own;
> And we magnify his strictness
> With a zeal he will not own.

While none of us can know what lies beyond death, it does at least seem reasonable to suppose that God's love remains unlimited and that he will provide himself with the means of continuing to express it to all those who still do not know the fullness of his grace. Indeed, only by doing so can there be that final *shalom*, order and harmony, which is creation's ultimate destiny.

But what are we to do with threat language—the weeping and gnashing of teeth? It would be a mistake to reject such language out of hand, to say simply that this is part of the Jewish ideas of the time and therefore no longer applicable for "man come of age". We must always beware of throwing out the baby with the bathwater. Rather what we should do is to accept the language as myth in the sense in which biblical scholars use that word—that is, that the language does not refer to something in the future but rather to something in the present, that heaven and hell are not specifically places of the hereafter but can be inhabited in the here and now. In other words, this language describes a present reality, just as that myth of our beginning describes the present reality of our condition—that we are sinners nakedly conscious of our alienation from God. God has, however, shown us that we do not have to remain in this position of alienation: rather, he wishes us to be his sons, and call him Abba, Father. The Old and New Testaments also show that to remain in separation from God can only lead to chaos, to wailing and gnashing of teeth as men and women exploit men and women for their own self-gratification. This is the message of the prophets: it is also the message of Paul. The decision that faces us is, then, vital and immediate: we are called now to turn to the God who wills to embrace us, and so enjoy his love, which is heaven indeed. The alternative is to stay eating the husks thrown to the pigs, which is hell. Recognised as myth, and transferred to the now, the language of heaven and hell has immediate relevance. It is like the rest of the biblical imagery which we associate with becoming a Christian—moving from death to life, from darkness to light. For it is the Christian conviction that only by responding to God's love can we achieve our true potential, our citizenship of heaven, which is ours to claim now.

So through the incarnation we discover the real nature of our relationship with God. In Jesus alone we find how much we matter to God, that whatever he does the arms of the crucified will not let us go. The picture then of the valley of dry bones is a picture not just for Israel, but for each individual, whoever he or she is, wherever he or she is, and whatever he or she has done, into whom the God of grace will yet breathe his recreating spirit. God is indeed Emmanuel, "God with us", for in the end he cannot be against us. This is the gospel. It *is* good news.

iv. Jesus and the Nature of Belief

In very similar circumstances to Job, Jesus is brought to the ultimate test. Like Job, he finds himself an outcast of the city. He is innocent of any fault, yet he is being made to suffer, apparently at the hands of the very God in whom he has utterly trusted and whom he has unflinchingly obeyed. And at the very moment when he is most needed, God remains agonisingly absent. He could of course have cursed God and died. He does not and lives. In the silence of the absence of God, Jesus is faced with Job's choice: to deny God or his own integrity. He does neither, but instead affirms both.

But Jesus' affirmation is no simple declaration of faith. He does not resign himself to his fate; instead he argues himself towards his seemingly inevitable death: "My God, my God, why have you forsaken me?" (Matthew 27:46; Mark 15:34). While in Gethsemane he was content to leave things to God, now on the cross, faced on the one hand by the reality of his imminent death and on the other with the loss of God's presence, and so of any explanation for what is going on, he, like Job and the Psalmist, hurls the hostile "why?" at the apparently indifferent God. Yet despite an unimaginable loneliness, his utter desolation, God is still "my God". For Jesus makes it unequivocally clear that it is God who is on trial: it is he who has "forsaken" Jesus. So Jesus continues to express his faith, but that faith is phrased as only a man can phrase it: "In spite of ... I believe". At the point where Jesus exhibits the fullness of his humanity, at his death, he also shows what being human means—that men and women cannot of necessity know all the answers, but that they can still believe. Yet they can only be agnostic believers, and that is no contradiction in terms, for that was what was ordained for them at creation.

From the earliest days, the Church identified Jesus as the meek suffering servant of Deutero-Isaiah. But we must beware of over literal identification. While it may be correct in the main to say:

> He was despised, shunned by all,
> pain-racked and afflicted by disease;
> we despised him, we held him of no account,
> an object from which people turn away their eyes.
>
> *Isaiah 53:3*

we cannot continue:

> He was maltreated, yet he was submissive
> and did not open his mouth;
> like a sheep led to the slaughter,
> like a ewe that is dumb before the shearers,
> he did not open his mouth.
>
> *Isaiah 53:7*

For Jesus' true humanity is not seen in a passionless exhibition of disinterested religion. Jesus is no meek Job of the Prologue, content to let events take their course come what may. Rather, like Job of the Dialogue, he wrestles with God and will not let God go until he answers him. But Jesus, unlike Job, has to carry that fight through the jaws of death itself. He has to do that most illogical of all acts, express faith at the point of apparent extinction. So the Light of the World is snuffed out with a question.

Yet like Job with his self-curse (Job 31), Jesus, by hanging on through death itself, forces God's hand. His plea cannot go unanswered: the trial must have a verdict. And that verdict is not that of the Jewish authorities or Pilate, who, like Job's friends, had condemned him. It is the verdict of God himself: "The curtain of the temple was torn in two from top to bottom" (Matthew 27:51). The Jewish authorities who claimed to know all the answers are condemned and Jesus vindicated. In his agonising cry from the cross, he has spoken correctly. He rises on the third day.

It is, then, the cry from the cross that confirms the reality of the incarnation: this was no charade. Jesus does not just go through the motions of what it means to be human: he lives his humanity out in ignorance, futility, and defeat. He shows that under the conditions obtaining in this world, God cannot always get his way. Good men and women do become victims of evil, suffer unjustly. But this is not to say that Jesus was a mere man—for once one encounters the truly human Jesus, one sees God. It is though as a man, with all man's limitations spelt out in Eden, that Jesus validates his divine nature.

v. The "Gospel" of the Bible

We have now seen that the New Testament confirms the Old, for it reveals the nature of the one unchanging God. His message is clear to us, though its simplicity still surprises: let God be God, and get on with being the men and women God created us to be. And increasingly in a world "come of age" we are able to do this as science unravels the facts and fantasies of human existence. But if we are to enjoy our humanity in all its fullness, we still need to be wise in the Old Testament sense of seeking that order and harmony which God willed for his world at its creation, so that wild and domestic animals can lie down together in peace (*shalom*) and children play in safety by snakes' nests (Isaiah 11).

Yet we all-too-readily refuse to embrace our natural humanity, shunning the physical, denying our flesh and blood. The Marxist jibe that Christians multiplied litanies and neglected drains nicely encapsulates this perversion. But what is the one commandment that Jesus gave us?—to love one another, and nothing is more physical than love. For to love demands, as any lover knows, our total involvement in the other—the very guts of our being. Men and women can only truly be themselves in the full earthiness of their physical nature. It is this essential earthiness that makes being human so frightening and from which so many draw back, seeking safety rather than engagement, often covering their fear in pious platitude.

Ibsen's hero, Brand, was a pastor driven by his conscience to ever-increasing self-denial and sacrifice to the God whom he sought to serve. Nothing was to stand in the way of his total commitment. Towards the end of the play, Brand is asked:

> First, how long shall we have to fight?
> Secondly, how much will it cost us?
> Thirdly, what will be our reward?

Brand's reply is uncompromising:

> How long will you have to fight? Until you die!
> What will it cost? Everything you hold dear.
> Your reward? A new will, cleansed and strong;

> A new faith, integrity of spirit;
> A crown of thorns. That will be your reward.

But Brand had made a terrible mistake. He had forgotten the nature of the God whom he sought to serve. Terribly, he had denied his own humanity, his own flesh and blood. In the furtherance of his ministry, he had allowed his son to die, then his wife—virtually murdered both of them—and now, as his own life is about to be engulfed in the falling avalanche on the mountain he had climbed, he cries in anguish:

> Answer me God, in the moment of death!
> If not by Will, how can man be redeemed?

The avalanche buries him, filling in the whole valley. A voice cries through the thunder: "He is the God of Love."

As men and women, we are to be that love—that love in the way in which God is love. And we know what that is, for God has expressed it through the incarnation, through becoming fully human. Our task then is not to be "other", more "beyond", not to go on endlessly up the mountain of denial as Brand did, becoming ever more inaccessible, more alone: no, our task is to stay in the valley down below where there are people, laughter and sunlight; and sin, suffering and healing too (Matthew 17:14–18; Mark 9:14–27; Luke 9:37–43). Our call is to sit at table with tarts and crooks and to worry over a widow's poverty. For only by love of life can we affirm life, and only by affirming life shall we be led to ensure that all men and women have the chance of enjoying that life.

We are, then, not summoned to a life of suffering and sacrifice, though that may come our way: rather we are invited to leave the desert with all its deprivations and enter the land of milk and honey, there to feast in plenty. No one loved life more than Jesus. They called him a glutton and a winebibber. For too long Christians have, with Brand, emphasised the safety of denial—but such a theology is as corrupting as the tables of the money-changers. It needs overturning. For what the world is waiting for is a faith which affirms, affirms the goodness of life, affirms love in the very guts of its belly. And it is only as we love life as it should be that we shall be sufficiently sensitive to appreciate all life's horrors. Sadly, there will always be those who in their luxury blind themselves to the needy, like Lazarus, at their feet. But that is no excuse for isolating oneself from all that being human involves. For unless we are in the world with all its inequality, we have no hope of ever exercising that love which God wills us to be. To affirm life is not to deny the cruelties, injustices, and sheer unfairness of so much that occurs in this world. Rather it is to enter into the cosmic battle to ensure that Christ's kingdom does come, comes in all its fullness.

Of course, there will be failure: David must strive in Bathsheba's arms; Peter deny his Lord. But then they can know the reality of the gracious God who has created them in love and will not let them go. God does not condemn those who fail: it is those who bury their talents for safety who find themselves flung into the dark, the place of wailing and grinding of teeth. For to be human always involves risks, and not all risks come off. But in an age seduced into the brothel of success, failure seems as catastrophic as castration. So men and women play for safety—but no ideal ever had safety for a parent.

And there is no greater ideal than to be human—really human—to love unconditionally. This is no well-intentioned humanism, for it means at the outset recognising oneself (and all others) as created by God. It can then only be achieved, as Jesus—the one perfect human—showed, by total fellowship with God, in utter dependence upon him. In this life we know that sin prevents us fully realising our perfection—yet the command remains: You must be holy, because I, the Lord your God, am holy (Leviticus 19:2). You shall be those who bring wholeness, harmony, and order in all that you do and say and think. For the land of milk and honey can only be entered if we co-operate with the God who wills our entry. Christians are not called to make a choice between God and the world. Rather they are to affirm both, and in fellowship with their Creator enjoy his creation, whose true order is theirs to discover and proclaim.

Chronology

Date	Event	Kings	Prophets
1000		David (1000–961)	Nathan
	On Solomon's death, separate kingdoms of Israel in the north (capital Samaria) and Judah in the south (capital Jerusalem)	Solomon (*c.*961–922)	

◆　　◆　　◆

Date	Event	Kings	Prophets
750			Amos Hosea
721	Fall of Samaria to Assyria and end of the northern kingdom of Israel	Hezekiah (715–687)	Isaiah Micah
621	Discovery of law book in the temple led to Deuteronomic reform	Josiah (640–609)	Jeremiah
586	Fall of Jerusalem, destruction of the temple, and exile in Babylon of king and leading citizens		Ezekiel
561	Release of Jehoiachin from prison		
538	Edict of Persian king, Cyrus, allowing Jews to return from exile		Deutero-Isaiah

Index of Biblical References

Old Testament

New Testament

9 781910 519837